Citizens' Power in Latin America

Citizens' Power in Latin America

Theory and Practice

Pascal Lupien

SUNY
PRESS

Published by State University of New York Press, Albany

For information, contact State University of New York Press, Albany, NY
www.sunypress.edu

Library of Congress Cataloging-in-Publication Data

Names: Lupien, Pascal, author.
Title: Citizens' power in Latin America : theory and practice / Pascal Lupien.
Description: Albany : State University of New York Press, 2018. | Includes
  bibliographical references and index.
Identifiers: LCCN 2017021781 (print) | LCCN 2017031377 (ebook) | ISBN
  9781438469195 (ebook) | ISBN 9781438469171 (hardcover   ) |
  ISBN 9781438469188 (pbk.   )
Subjects: LCSH: Political participation—Latin America. | Citizens' advisory
  committees—Latin America. | Political participation—Venezuela. | Citizens'
  advisory committees—Venezuela. | Political participation—Ecuador. | Citizens'
  advisory committees—Ecuador. | Political participation—Chile. | Citizens' advisory
  committees—Chile.
Classification: LCC JL966 (ebook) | LCC JL966 .L86 2018 (print) | DDC
  323/.042098—dc23
LC record available at https://lccn.loc.gov/2017021781

10 9 8 7 6 5 4 3 2 1

Contents

Tables

Acknowledgments

First and foremost, I would like to express my appreciation to Jordi Díez, Janine Clark, Leah Levac, and Kerry Preibisch for the time, patience, dedication, and advice they provided throughout the research and writing process. Their guidance was invaluable at all stages of the development of this research project. My sincere thanks also go to Tulia Falleti, Professor of Political Science at the University of Pennsylvania, for contributing her expertise and insightful questions to the final examination process. The knowledge, expertise, and high expectations of these academics have resulted in a stronger book. I must also thank a number of other scholars who have provided various forms of support and encouragement over the past five years: Candace Johnson, Gordana Yovanovich, Roberta Rice, Jorge Nef, Craig Johnson, Byron Sheldrick, David MacDonald, Adam Sneyd, Edward Koning, Tamara Small, and Rosario Gómez. I am also grateful to the staff of the Department of Political Science at the University of Guelph for their dedication and willingness to solve problems and address concerns. I would also like to thank my editor, Dr. Michael Rinella, the peer reviewers, and the staff at SUNY Press, particularly Eileen Nizer and Anne Valentine, for their attention to detail and invaluable feedback.

This research was carried out in three amazing countries: Venezuela, Chile, and Ecuador, my beloved adopted land that holds a special place in my heart. I am fortunate to have had the opportunity to meet so many fascinating, dynamic people who are dedicated to the improvement of democracy in their countries. I would like to express my deep gratitude to all those who offered their time and perspectives. For their help and the contacts they provided, a special thanks to Franklin Ramírez (FLACSO Ecuador); Maria Amelia Viteri (San Francisco University of Quito); Steve Ellner (Universidad de Oriente, Venezuela); Rossana Castiglioni (Universidad Diego Portales, Santiago); and Robert Funk (Institute of Public Affairs, University of Chile).

This book is dedicated to the people of Tarqui in Manta, Ecuador, one of the neighborhoods studied in this book. Many lives were lost or disrupted, and many homes and business were destroyed by an earthquake that devastated the Ecuadorian coast on April 16, 2016. I sincerely wish the people of Tarqui the best in rebuilding their community and their lives.

PART I

PARTICIPATORY DEMOCRACY IN THEORY AND PRACTICE

1

Introduction

The Emergence of Democratic Institutional Innovation in Latin America

In the past decade, Latin America has witnessed an explosion of institutions designed to encourage and channel popular participation in decision-making. In neighborhoods and communities across the region, average citizens are experimenting with innovative ways of deepening democracy. Citizens who have never been politically active and people from traditionally marginalized groups are engaging in participatory processes that are having an impact on their communities. Some are building housing projects using local labor while others are repairing deteriorating infrastructure in their neighborhoods. Parents are having a say in remodeling their children's schools and equipping them with sports facilities and kitchens. Domestic workers who must make the long daily trek from their low-income barrios to the homes of their employers have been involved in creating new bus routes that shorten their daily commutes.

These are a few of the more positive examples of how citizens who have been ignored by decision makers in the past are taking matters into their own hands through the new participatory architecture that is emerging in Latin America. Participatory mechanisms have flourished under left-wing governments that claim a strong ideological commitment to "radical" participatory democracy, while in other countries citizen participation is promoted as a pragmatic means of improving governance rather than as an alternative model of democratic politics. These developments have led some scholars to argue that the center of democratic innovation has moved from North to South and that we have a great deal to learn by studying these initiatives.

There is considerable variation, however, in terms of how participatory mechanisms function from one neighborhood to the next. In some cases, marginalized residents are achieving improved access to public goods and services and developing a stronger sense of political efficacy. They see a powerful link between citizen participation and more equitable outcomes than those provided by traditional representative institutions. In other cases, the picture is less promising. Residents do not feel empowered and continue to find themselves excluded from the political process. What explains these differences in outcomes? Why do some democratic innovations appear to succeed while others fail? Does the "radical" participatory democracy model implemented by administrations that seek to overturn traditional power structures provide more significant benefits than the more pragmatic experiments aimed at improving governance through limited citizen participation?

This book answers these questions by examining participatory mechanisms in three countries through the eyes of the women and men who devote their time and energy to improving their communities. Why are these participatory innovations important? Liberal democracy is facing a crisis of legitimacy around the world, and particularly in Latin America. According to the 2015 Latinobarometer report, only 39% of Latin Americans were satisfied with the quality of democracy in their country. Perhaps even more troublesome is the low level of support for democracy in Latin America, with nearly half of the region's citizens claiming that democracy is not necessarily the best form of government. Political institutions are failing to meet the aspirations of increasing numbers of citizens. The high level of public dissatisfaction with the current state of democracy has reignited the debate surrounding the most effective means of integrating popular participation into the policy process. Politicians, non-governmental organizations (NGOs), students of democracy and concerned citizens are thinking about innovative ways of deepening democracy. In order to engage in this discussion, we must develop a better understanding of the strengths and weaknesses of participatory mechanisms.

This book contributes to this important discussion by looking at a particular type of participatory innovation that has emerged across Latin America: local citizens' councils that provide individuals with the opportunity to engage in the decision-making process at the neighborhood level in an institutionalized environment. It compares participatory mechanisms in three countries with different models of participatory design: Venezuela's radical participatory democracy, which claims to replace liberal representative institutions with grassroots direct democracy at the local level; Chile's pragmatic efforts at expanding participation for the purposes of achieving more efficient governance and enhancing liberal institutions; and Ecuador's hybrid model that demonstrates features of both.

The following chapters enhance our knowledge on citizen participation in several ways. This is one of the first studies to examine participatory mechanisms from both a cross-country and within-country perspective. Most research has focused on either unique case studies or on within-country comparisons. It is the first to study the new "radical" participatory mechanisms in countries such as Venezuela and Ecuador in comparative perspective and to contrast these with different, more "pragmatic" models of participatory design. It also draws on original qualitative evidence and connects the readers to citizens who participate in these institutions. The book takes the reader into the heart of neighborhoods where marginalized citizens are attempting to use these institutions to improve their communities and have a voice in decisions that affect their lives. We will meet citizen participants from across these three countries, learn about the successes and failures they have experienced through their participatory processes, and hear about their hopes and frustrations.

Methods and Cases

This book uncovers the conditions that make participatory democracy successful across different models of institutional design through a two-level comparison. It compares local participatory mechanisms across three countries (and therefore across three models of institutional design) and also compares three cases within each country. This innovative two-level design allows us to transcend the usual within-country comparison approach to look at the impact of different models of institutional design and government discourse on participatory democracy, as well as the factors that enhance or diminish the capacity of these mechanisms to achieve positive outcomes within and across models of institutional design.

Considering similar institutions in different countries allows us to understand to what extent the design of participatory mechanisms and government commitment to citizen participation matters. It helps to determine which variables produce benefits, which are less relevant and which are more likely to lead to failure. Comparing institutions based on radical participatory democracy with a case of "liberal" participatory institutions that are similar in functions and objectives but based on more pragmatic principles is useful in testing some of the variables. For example, radical democrats view participation as an alternative to representation, so it is valuable to consider whether participatory institutions that work more closely with government (as one of the conditions) are more or less effective than those that are entirely autonomous.

The cases of Venezuela and Ecuador were selected to provide a strong and informative comparison for a number of reasons. Of the recent attempts at creating institutions to channel participation, the new institutions in these countries are arguably the most directly associated with the principles of radical democracy, including a rejection of neoliberalism and representative democracy (Burbach and Piñero 2007; Ellner 2010; Hawkins 2010 and also see Venezuela 2006, 2009; Ecuador 2010). They are comparable in that they have similar local-level institutions and these have been promoted through a similar ideological framework. In terms of institutional design, they demonstrate (at least on paper) many of the characteristics identified by theorists as essential for participatory democracy to work, including "bottom-up" design, autonomy from state authorities, decision-making powers as opposed to merely consultative prerogatives, deliberative forums for discussion and debate, and links with higher levels of government (MacPherson 1977; Poulantzas 1978; Barber 1984; Cohen 1997; Fung and Wright 2003; Cohen and Rogers 2003).

Chile was selected as a case against which to compare and test the other two. Generally cited in the literature as one of the least participatory countries in Latin America, it is seen as a model of liberal representative democracy in the region (Cameron, Hershberg and Sharpe 2012). There has been a marked shift in discourse from 2000 onward, however. The first administration of President Michelle Bachelet (2006–2010) declared increased citizen participation to be an important goal, although participation in the Chilean context tends to be framed as an instrument for effective governance and policymaking and not as an alternative to representative democracy (Cleuren 2007; Chile 2011). The past few years have seen concrete changes including the adoption of a new national law that recognizes citizen participation as a right and provides stronger legal recognition and support to institutions such as the *juntas de vecinos* (neighbourhood councils) (Chile 2011).

Within-country comparisons allow us to delve even further into understanding why some participatory innovations are more successful than others and also help to confirm patterns observed at the cross-country level. They allow us to determine whether the same factors that emerge as important in affecting outcomes between participatory design models also turn up when comparing mechanisms in the same country. This allows us to uncover any "universal" factors that are important in the design of participatory mechanisms, and to what extent institutional design and government discourse (radical or pragmatic) on participatory democracy play a role in determining outcomes. It also allows us to consider the impact of local contextual factors on the ability of participatory mechanisms to achieve positive outcomes.

This study employs a subnational comparative case study design that allows for in-depth description and comparisons of instances of citizen participation. This is a useful approach to evaluating the outcomes of participatory processes as it helps the researcher to use a number of qualitative data collection methods designed to develop a detailed understanding of processes, outcomes, and participant experiences (Nabatchi 2012). Subnational comparisons are an efficient way to construct controlled comparisons when the number of cases involved is low and facilitates both within and across-country comparison (Avritzer 2009; Snyder, 2001). The approach is also particularly useful for studying context, which is essential to understanding the conditions under which participatory institutions operate.

To the extent possible, this study has looked at a representative sample of participatory institutions in each country, selecting cases according to a diverse case method to achieve a certain level of variation on a number of important dimensions (Seawright and Gerring 2008; Altschuler and Corrales 2012). Local participatory mechanisms were selected to reflect population distribution as well as a number of other factors: important regional/cultural differences, ethnic representation, political cleavages, socioeconomic factors, and the urban vs. rural divide. In Venezuela, interviews were conducted with participants in communal councils in Caracas (Catia), a semi-rural council in Yagua, Carabobo State, and one in the interior city of Mérida (Belém). In Ecuador, it was important to capture both the highlands and coast as the population is divided more or less evenly between these two regions, which also have represented the primary political and cultural divisions in the country. Cases include a local assembly outside of Quito (Llano Chico), a rural assembly from the northern highlands (San Gabriel), and one from an urban district in the mid-sized coastal city of Manta (Tarqui). Regional differences have not been as historically significant in Chile but socioeconomic divisions run deep.

Two cases were selected from the greater Santiago area (medium-income Maipú and low-income La Pintana) and one from Valdivia in southern Chile (semi-urban Cayumapú).

The research was conducted over a nine-month period, from September 2012 to May 2013, with follow-up visits in July–August 2014 and June–July 2015. As mentioned earlier, one of the goals of this research was to study participatory mechanisms from the perspective of the citizens themselves. Answering the research questions posed in this book required a thorough understanding of citizens' lived experiences. It was also necessary to develop a clear picture of their goals, the participatory processes, outcomes and state-society interactions in order to fully comprehend the "chains of sovereignty" between citizens, participatory mechanisms and state actors (Baiocchi, Heller and Silva 2011).

Data includes semi-structured interviews and documents produced by the participatory mechanisms and by relevant local and central government departments. A total of 222 semi-structured interviews were conducted. Citizens engaged in participatory mechanisms accounted for 136 of these (49 Venezuela, 46 Ecuador, 41 Chile). These interviews focused on the tangible benefits of participation, the processes to achieve these outcomes and on the conditions under which the participatory mechanisms operate.

Another 86 interviews were conducted with government officials, opposition actors and academics. Government authorities generally fall into two categories: (1) Senior and mid-level officials in departments and agencies responsible for implementing participatory policies or with oversight of participatory institutions, and (2) Local (generally municipal) officials from the communes and parishes in which the cases studied are located.

This research was complemented by studying various types of documents produced by the local participatory mechanisms themselves, and by local and central government departments. Examples of documents analyzed include: documents produced by each participatory mechanism, project proposals and planning documents, evaluation reports, budget documents showing money received, community oversight reports, and documents produced by agencies charged with supporting and funding public participation initiatives and training.

There are a number of challenges that must be acknowledged. Given that the book looks at public goods (infrastructure development) before and after the existence of participatory mechanisms in each locale, there was to some extent a need to rely on the memory and perceptions of participants and public officials with respect to the role that participation played in achieving any tangible benefits. Participants were asked about what their participatory mechanisms had achieved. While participant perceptions are routinely used to measure the outcomes of participatory processes, critics have pointed to the problems associated with interpreting such data and have argued that satisfaction is not necessarily indicative of "good" policy (Abelson and Gauvin 2006). To some extent, this problem was offset by the fact there was considerable consensus in most cases around this question, and the researcher only recorded a project as a benefit of participation when a clear majority of participants identified it and tied it to the efforts of their citizens' council. Triangulation was also used whenever possible. In addition to asking participants, local officials and a number of nonparticipants or former participants were asked the same questions to determine if they also attributed a given infrastructure project to the local citizens' council or to some other factor(s). Wherever possible, the researcher used available documentation (project plans, budget information) to back up the information provided by informants (i.e., do municipal planning or budget documents also attribute given projects to the participatory mechanism?).

Establishing causal links between participation in these institutions and particular outcomes remains a challenge due to various spurious variables, the time-lag between processes and outcomes and the impact of intervening events over time. Determining the counterfactual is also problematic as it is not possible to demonstrate what the outcomes would have been without the participatory process. While there are obvious diffi-culties in demonstrating causal links between participation and outcomes, the methods employed in a case study design can produce "most likely" correlations between processes and outcomes (Barrett, Wyman and Coelho, 2012). Researchers and practitioners who study public participation argue that case studies relying on qualitative data can make strong "logical links" between a participatory experience and policy impacts, although these are based on "most likely associations" rather than on direct causal links (Nabatchi, 2012; Barrett, Wyman and Coelho, 2012).

Arguments

The following chapters demonstrate that popular participation can have an important impact on communities and on individual citizens under the right circumstances. Participatory mechanisms have produced significant tangible outcomes at the local level, such as more equitable access to public goods and services. Some cases also generate promising spillover effects, such as more positive perceptions of democracy and enhanced sense of political efficacy among participants. While these outcomes are observable to some extent in most of the participatory mechanisms studied in this book, there is significant variation between the three countries and among the nine cases. The mere existence of citizen participation mechanisms in a given community does not guarantee positive outcomes. A number of characteristics have an impact on the capacity of participatory mechanisms to produce positive outcomes. These include: quality of deliberation (can everyone participate or are the participatory mechanisms dominated by certain groups?); inclusiveness (do the mechanisms really include the formerly excluded or simply act as another forum for the middle sectors to promote their interests?), and high levels of participation and engagement (proportion of the community that participates regularly and how committed they are to participation). Both among and within the three countries, these characteristics are observable in those cases that produce better outcomes and practically absent in the mechanisms that do not fare as well.

Effective working relationships between participatory mechanisms and local authorities are also key, particularly when the formal decision-making powers of the participatory mechanisms are limited, as in Ecuador and Chile. Full devolution of decision-making and implementation powers is mostly associated with the radical Venezuelan model. This does produce positive tangible outcomes, but participants working within the pragmatic model with comparatively limited formal powers can find ways of getting what they want by using their mechanisms to develop effective (even if not always cordial) relationships with local officials, or to persuade them.

The "radical" model, with its promises of deepening the quality of democracy, has both strengths and weaknesses. State discourse on participatory democracy does not necessarily have a significant impact on the ability of participatory mechanisms to produce positive outcomes. Citizens are more likely to achieve tangible outcomes, however, when the discourse behind participatory mechanisms aligns with the reality of how they function. In both Venezuela and Chile, participatory discourse produced by the state along with the relevant enabling legislation align to a significant degree with how the mechanisms actually work. This shapes participants' expectations and strategies in engaging with their participatory institutions. In Ecuador, there is a notable disconnect between state discourse and legislation on the one hand, and how the institutions function in reality, on the other. This produces tension between participants and local authorities as citizens' expectations of what their participatory mechanisms should do are not realized in their day-to-day operation. This tension damages the relationship between participants and local authorities, thus further reducing the role of the former in decision making and implementation.

State discourse and institutional design can also have negative (intended or unintended) consequences. Participatory institutions can provide significant opportunities for actors—particularly those from traditionally marginalized sectors—to engage in meaningful decision making to an extent that is rarely seen elsewhere, including in more developed democracies. They allow these actors to exercise a degree of agency that was denied to them under traditional political structures. The danger is that design of these institutions creates relationships with the state that may simultaneously promote more inclusive decision making while establishing parameters around democratic participation. Civil society organizations (as well as individuals) may only effectively exercise this newfound agency through state-sanctioned channels. The intention of "radical" participatory mechanisms may be to strengthen civil society and citizenship as agency, but the design of these mechanisms may tip the balance toward controlled inclusion. Furthermore, the benefits of institutionalized citizen participation are limited to influence in decision making at the local level. This is the case across the three countries and is observed in both the radical and pragmatic models. While we can see examples of civil society engaging in the political process independent of local government in some cases, in none of the cases does this extend to regional or national levels.

With these important caveats in mind, participatory mechanisms produce the most positive outcomes when they are inclusive, demonstrate a high quality of internal deliberation, foster a significant level of sustained engagement, and either enjoy a real devolution of decision-making powers or develop effective working relationships with local officials.

Organization of the Book

Chapter 2 provides the relevant theoretical and analytical framework to understand participatory theory, the benefits that participation are supposed to produce, and how we can evaluate them, as well as the gaps in our knowledge that the book addresses. Chapter 3 provides the relevant historical and political context surrounding the emergence of participatory institutions in the three countries and outlines the two models that have emerged.

Part II draws on interviews with citizen participants and public officials as well as document analysis to tell the story of these models of citizen participation. In chapter 4, the reader meets participants from Venezuelan communal councils, the prototype for the "radical" participatory democracy model in Latin America. Chapter 5 looks at Ecuador's local citizens' assemblies, while chapter 6 introduces the reader to Chile's neighbourhood councils. The final chapter concludes by discussing the broader implications of this study's findings for our understanding of participatory democracy. These include the strengths that have been identified in the book as well as some worrying trends. The chapter ends with what all of this can teach us about the effective design of participatory institutions.

2

Theoretical Origins of Citizen Participation

Democracy as an Essentially Contested Concept

Debates surrounding the appropriate role of the public in decision making can be traced back to Ancient Greece and continue to mark the Latin American landscape today. These disputes revolve around the value of mass participation vs. representation by elite groups, participation as a tool for development and problem solving, the existence of a common good or general will, individual freedom vs. equality, and the maintenance of order vs. an expanded role for "the masses" in decision making.

Democracy must be understood as an "essentially contested concept" in that its meaning is constantly and will likely always be subject to dispute and debate (Gallie 1956). Although there is far more complexity than a simple dichotomy can fully account for, many theorists suggest that conceptions of democracy can be divided into two main camps: direct-participative and liberal-representative (Held 2006). The first group argues that democracy must be expanded and deepened, that participation in politics promotes self-development and more equitable outcomes, and that government is only legitimate when the governed are involved in decision making. The second group believes that most people are either incapable of making good decisions or not interested in political participation and that in any case, too much participation can lead to instability and even tyranny. They favor the rule of law and elite representatives elected by the people who can aggregate demands, rather than direct popular rule. While theoretical debates about the nature of democracy persist in the academic literature, in the public sphere the dominant discourse privileges the liberal representative model over others to the extent that many come to equate democracy with this variant (Fung and Wright 2003).

Many of the ideals of Athenian democracy (and the criticisms of its detractors) have influenced thinking in the West throughout the centuries. Despite its highly restricted participation (which excluded women, slaves, and non-citizens), the basic principles of Athenian democracy have continued to inspire those who value participation in decision making. The question of popular participation reemerged as a significant topic of debate among intellectuals in the eighteenth and nineteenth centuries. Jean-Jacques Rousseau (1994 [1762]) produced what was for his time a radical view on citizenship and has been called the theorist "par excellence" of participatory democracy (Pateman 1970). Rousseau opposed the idea that people should be governed uniquely through elected representatives, in the form of a parliament or other legislative body. He believed in the individual participation of all citizens in decision making and viewed participation as central to the establishment and maintenance of a democratic system. Rousseau was concerned about the dominance of individual interests and believed that citizen participation in a context of relative socioeconomic equality was the best way to ensure that the "general will" would take precedence over selfish private interests (Rousseau 1994 [1762]). Rousseau's conception of democracy would inspire the thinking of participatory democrats in the twentieth century and up to the present day and its theoretical ideals are embedded in the participatory institutions of twenty-first-century Latin America (Selee and Peruzzotti 2009).

Liberal democracy and its generally more constrained and elitist notions around the extent of popular participation would challenge Rousseauian conceptions of democracy. Liberalism emphasizes values of individual freedom and personal choice, and freedom of private interests from political interference (the notion of protective democracy). The concept of a general will or common good is generally dismissed (Nelson 2006). The growing bourgeoisie of the seventeenth and eighteenth centuries was understandably attracted to concepts of individual rights and popular sovereignty. Many twentieth-century theorists of representative democracy are influenced by the work of Joseph Schumpeter. Looking back at what he calls "classical" democratic thinkers, Schumpeter (1942) argues that it is not possible for "the people" to rule with the exception of small and "primitive" societies with a simple social structure. Schumpeter and his followers do not see participation as a desirable objective. He accuses people of being prone to "poor judgement" and "irrational impulses" and inclined to use "weak logic" to analyze complex matters that are simply beyond them (Schumpeter 1942: 260–263). We must therefore, he argues, replace the unrealistic notion of government by the people with government approved by the people.

A growing number of theorists from the 1970s onward have rejected the minimalist view and have developed theories that challenge this hegemonic model. These critics of representative democracy have attempted to apply some of Rousseau's ideas in a contemporary context. It is in these ideas that we find the theoretical inspiration for the experiments in participatory democracy currently flourishing in Latin America and elsewhere. While there is considerable variety among the different perspectives, proponents of "radical democracy" share a sharp criticism of the exclusionary nature of representative institutions as they have functioned in practice and a desire to broaden and deepen democracy through the creation of institutions that allow for citizen participation and deliberation. Radical democrats call for "more participatory-deliberative mechanisms that give citizens a direct role in decision making and challenge "conventional" (liberal representative) democracy (Cohen and Fung 2004).

In her concise but influential work, Pateman (1970) criticized what she referred to as the contemporary theories of minimalist democracy. Pateman rejects that the "masses" are ignorant and uninterested in politics, that participation should be limited to voting, and that elected elites should be left to make decisions. She believes that "representative" democracy is not really representative and argues that participation is a common good in itself. MacPherson (1977) also emphasizes the need for extensive citizen participation in government. He offers a strong critique of liberal democracy, arguing that proponents confuse democracy with free markets and insisting that this leads to the "freedom of the stronger to do down the weaker following market rules." Barber dismisses the liberal model as "thin democracy" which acts as "the chambermaid of private interests" and goes so far as to argue that the term "representative democracy" is an oxymoron (Barber 1984: 117). More recently, Santos and Avritzer (2005) argue that the struggle for democracy today is above all a struggle for the democratization of democracy. This must include an acceptance of "demo-diversity" (the recognition that there are many variants of democratic practice and the rejection of the Western drive to impose its hegemonic model on the South) and a rejection of "low intensity" representative democracy through increased participation. Writing in the Latin American context, Van Cott understands radical democracy as "normative theory that proposes alternative—sometimes utopian—norms and process that aim to significantly improve the quality of democratic life" (Van Cott 2008: 8–9).

Much of the contemporary literature on democracy in Latin America has focused on democratic consolidation (or lack thereof) at the national level following the Third Wave of democratic transitions that swept the region in the 1970s and 1980s. More recently, some scholars have criticized the earlier literature for focusing exclusively on procedural issues and paying little attention to substantive matters, such as the quality of democracy. For O'Donnell (2004), a democratic regime is essential but not sufficient for real democracy. He acknowledges that studying the substantive elements is "tricky," but argues that it is essential to do so. Agency is the grounding factor of democracy and allows us to assess the differential quality of actually existing democracies. Hagopian (2005, 2007) also argues that the literature has looked at "democracy without citizens." She encourages a shift in the research agenda from democratic consolidation to a focus on substantive issues such as the quality of democracy, arguing that studying political institutions without considering the aspirations of a country's citizens is no longer adequate.

Citizen Participation: Potential Benefits and Designing Mechanisms to Achieve Them

While few authors believe that liberal institutions can or should be done away with, most point to the failures of these "minimalist" arrangements and argue that enhanced citizen participation can lead to better outcomes for a greater number of people. The potential outcomes are perhaps the most widely written about aspect of participatory democracy yet until recently there has been little empirical evidence to back up theorists' claims. While these are not conceived of as mutually exclusive, authors have tended to focus on either tangible outcomes or spillover effects. The first category focuses on results that improve the material conditions of those who have traditionally been excluded from the institutions through which decisions are made. A number of authors agree that participatory democracy should lead to more equitable policy outcomes, particularly greater access to public goods and services for marginalized sectors, including the poor, women, and ethnic minorities (Santos 1998; Avritzer 2002;

Santos and Avritzer 2005; Cohen and Fung 2004; Goldfrank 2011). These scholars contend that deepening democracy will, among other things, lead to a higher quality of life through redistributing resources in favor of the more vulnerable social groups, increased investment in the poorer districts, and improved public works projects in previously neglected areas. As we shall see in the following chapter, the discourse of state institutions in Venezuela and Ecuador with respect to public participation draws heavily on the concepts espoused by the tradition represented by these authors.

The second category focuses on the soft outcomes, often referred to in the literature as "spillover effects" of citizen participation (Altschuler and Corrales 2012). While there are various perspectives represented in this participatory democracy literature, a common criticism is that while the minimalist or "low intensity" representative model produces a disengaged citizenry and cynical perceptions of democracy itself, direct involvement in decision making leads to an improved perception of the legitimacy of democracy and an increased sense of political efficacy among participants (Macpherson 1977; Barber 1984; Baiocchi 2003; Wampler 2007; Smith 2009; Hellinger 2011). There have been various attempts over the past few decades to consider these types of effects of participation on citizens.

While not participatory democrats, Almond and Verba (1963) took the sense of political efficacy acquired by citizens as an operational effect of citizen participation that can be studied. They found a correlation between participation in organizations and sense of efficacy and concluded that participation may give people "skills needed to engage in political participation." Arnold Kaufman (1960), credited with coining the term "participatory democracy," wrote that democratic participation would improve participants' "powers of thought, feeling and action." Pateman (1970) posits that the more an individual participates in decision making (at home, in the workplace, or in the political arena), the greater his or her sense of political efficacy. Involvement at the local level is seen as a good place to begin; participation in local decision making is a means of "learning democracy," as it fosters "psychological qualities" required for participation at the national level as well as the development and practice of "democratic skills." Fearon (1998) elaborates further on the benefits of deliberation. Among other things, he believes that it can render decisions legitimate in the eyes of the group, improve the moral or intellectual capacities of participants, and produce the best decisions for the greatest numbers of people. Others have acknowledged that even where participation does not have a significant impact on policy outcomes, the possibility of recognition and having a voice may be an important benefit in and of itself (Font and Smith 2013).

Some authors have theorized about both sets of outcomes. Joshua Cohen, one of the strongest proponents of deliberative democracy, also draws on Habermas in developing the concept of public fora, or spaces for public forms of deliberation that produce binding decisions and lead to clear outcomes (Cohen 1997). Empowering citizens is seen as both an intrinsic good as well as a more efficient way of addressing tangible problems, but this can only come through deliberation that gives careful and serious weighing of reasons for and against a proposition (Cohen and Rogers 2003). Richardson (1983) provides a useful framework that encompasses both types of benefits identified by scholars, dividing these between developmental (the impact on participants, including increased self-esteem) and instrumental (improving the quality of decisions and policy outcomes).

If participatory mechanisms are to provide these types of "hard" and "soft" benefits, how must they be designed (or how they must the work in practice) in order to deliver on these promises? While they identify various characteristics, most authors agree that successful participatory mechanisms must demonstrate democratic procedural qualities, inclusiveness, the ability to influence the policy process, as well as sufficient independence from the state apparatus so that citizens do not lose their autonomy in the process (Font and Smith 2013; Font and Galais 2011; Cunill 2007). Barber (1984) proposes a number of criteria for the types of institutions he believes could promote and operationalize his vision of "strong democracy." They must be autonomous and have real decision-making powers, yet must also have a relationship with national or regional institutions so that local participation is linked to central power. They also require a base of committed citizens interested in deepening democracy and willing to invest the time and effort.

Cohen (1997), Fung and Wright (2003), and Cohen and Rogers (2003) offer more detailed prescriptions for institutional design "to bring real world institutions closer to utopian ideals." For them, deliberation must take place among equal citizens and involve the exercise of real authority as a means of transforming preferences from private to public in a way that would enhance possibilities for social cooperation. Their principles for institutional design include: bottom-up participation, real deliberation in which every citizen has an opportunity to have her voice heard, delegation of real power to the local level, "coordinated decentral-ization" which maintains linkages with higher levels to ensure that there are real policy outcomes based on the decisions of local actors, and state sponsorship of the institutions (as opposed to disconnected, volunteeristic initiatives) so that the institutional reforms actually transform the state by institutionalizing participation.

Fung and Wright (2003) provide researchers with a blueprint to help them study participatory institutions. They suggest a number of questions for researchers to consider when studying participatory democracy initia-tives. In terms of whether the institutions conform to theoretical princi-ples: Are there concrete outcomes and are these outcomes more desirable than those of prior and/or alternative institutional arrangements? To what extent do they constitute schools for democracy and increase capacities of participants? Do they improve quality of life through, for example, better access to public goods and services? How genuinely deliberative are the decision-making processes? How effectively are the decisions made through this process translated into action? To what extent can the deliberative bodies effectively monitor the implementation of their decisions?

Two Models of Participatory Design: Radical and Pragmatic

Over the past decade, we have witnessed the emergence of two different modes of participatory design in Latin America. In the first, and most common, participation is designed with pragmatic goals in mind, seeking to enhance (not replace) representation and provide better governance through citizen involvement in decision making (Oxhorn 1995; Montambeault 2011; Nylen 2011; Cleuren 2007). Institutions have been created or re-invigorated in recent years with the intention of enhancing governance and bringing citizens closer to their elected representatives. While not subscribing to the radical democracy ideals as discussed in the theoretical literature, these governments nonetheless support participatory mechanisms which liberal democrats claim will produce a deeper and richer democracy (Nylen 2011; Montambeaut 2011; Selee and Peruzzotti 2009). The discourse of popular participation has even become fashionable in Chile, often considered a model of representative democracy in the region but one of the least par-ticipatory systems (Cameron, Hershberg and Sharpe 2012).

Meanwhile, the vision championed by Venezuelan President Hugo Chávez (1999–2013) and Ecuadorian President Rafael Correa (2007–2017) goes beyond promoting more effective governance but is rooted in a "power to the people" discourse that is critical of liberal democracy and paints popular participation as more legitimate, at least at the local level (Méndez and Jonnathan 2009; Ellner 2010, 2012; Hawkins 2010; Irazábal and Foley 2010). This has created a direct challenge to Western hegemonic constructions of democracy imposed by the United States and local elites (Burron 2012). The radical participatory democracy model is character-ized by two elements: participatory rhetoric on the part of state actors (often couched in populist language) and the creation or modification of concrete institutions that leaders claim will translate this vision into practice (Ramírez and Welp 2011; Schnieder and Welp 2011; Goldfrank 2011b; Crespo 2008). The institutions range from national constitutional changes that establish citizen participation as a democratic right to the local mechanisms that we will study in part II.

Not surprisingly, serious criticisms have been levelled against "radical" participatory initiatives. Observers express concern that they will diminish the autonomy of civil society by co-opting individuals and organizations through state-supported initiatives (Lovera 2008; García-Guadilla 2008; Machado 2009). Participatory mechanisms could be used to create new forms of controlled inclusion similar to that of the corporatist regimes that dominated parts of Latin America in the twentieth century (McCarthy 2012). The proponents of radical democracy may in fact intend some of the dangers identified. For example, many proponents of radical democ-racy would not necessarily see the diminishing power of representative institutions (which are deemed unrepresentative) in a negative light. However, some of the dangers would, if they are in fact produced by the new institutions, conflict with radical democracy theory and would be a real cause for concern for radical democrats. These include the possibility that participatory institutions will simply reproduce class hierarchies in that those with higher levels of education (likely to be more "eloquent") will have significant advantages in a deliberative process (Bourdieu 1991), that social inequalities will exclude underprivileged minorities regardless of participatory mechanisms (Elstub and McLaverty 2014; Bonham 1996), or that most citizens will not be motivated to engage, either because they do not have the time or because they fail to see the benefit of doing so (Warren 1996; Lijphart 199; Mansbridge 1980). Others see a more complex relationship in which the form of populist mobilization we have seen in Venezuela may not be entirely incompatible with genuine participatory democracy (Hetland 2014; Lupien 2016).

Participatory Mechanisms: Gaps in the Research

While both supporters and opponents of radical democracy make strong theoretical arguments, many have noted that this literature tends to be abstract and generally fails to offer concrete examples or empirical evidence (Humphreys, Masters and Sandbu 2002; Cohen and Rogers 2003; Fung and Wright 2003; Delli Carpini, Cook and Jacobs 2004; Montero and Samuels 2004; Fung 2007; Van Cott 2008; Smith 2009). Conversely, little of the empirical work that does examine institutional innovations has directly addressed radical democracy theory (Baiocchi 2003). Beetham (1999) attributes this to a "disciplinary divorce" within political science between those who study political institutions and those who theorize about the principles of democracy. There is a clear and often noted need to address this gap by engaging in empirical research to determine to what extent participatory institutions conform to the theoretical principles. Fung (2007) believes that the lack of empirical research poses a "fundamental obstacle to progress in democratic theory." According to him, democratic theorists have successfully pointed out the limitations of liberal representative institutions and developed convincing arguments in favor of deeper democracy, but we cannot advance this theory further without studying the potential and real outcomes of actual institutions that promote citizen participation. Writing in the South American context, Van Cott (2008) also contends that the literature on radical democracy tends to be abstract, fails to offer concrete examples, and insists there is a need to address limitations of normative radical democracy literature by testing against empirical research.

In response to the explosion of participatory initiatives in Latin America, an increasing number of studies have started to address the emerging participatory discourse and institutional architecture in the region. One of the genuinely participatory experiments that has been the object of extensive empirical research is the Porto Alegre participatory budgeting model. A number of authors who have studied the Porto Alegre model argue that it can produce the benefits of participation identified in the theoretical literature (Santos 1998; Avritzer 2002, 2009; Abers 2000; Baiocchi 2003; Goldfrank 2011). A few works present in-depth case studies of participatory mechanisms in countries such as Brazil and Mexico. These authors generally find mixed results in terms of the outcomes achieved and effectiveness of these initiatives (Selee 2009; Selee and Peruzzotti 2009; Montambeault 2011; Cameron, Hershberg and Sharpe 2012). While the number of studies has increased in recent years, research has tended to focus overwhelmingly on case studies and there is a marked lack of comparative research (Smith 2009). While studies focused on countries such as Brazil have produced within-country comparisons, across-country comparisons and studies that combine comparisons of participatory initiatives both within and across countries are lacking (Montambeault 2015).

Goldfrank (2011) does engage in comparative research among three South American cities, but his work focuses on mechanisms developed at the municipal (rather than the national) level and was conducted prior to the election of the left-leaning governments in countries such as Venezuela and the emergence of the "radical" model and discourse on "citizen's power." Comparing within and across Brazil and Mexico, Montambeault (2015) examines the nature of state-society relationships produced by these initiatives and the factors that determine to what extent they are able to create positive relationships that allow civil society to effectively engage in local decision making. This research provides important new insights into what makes participatory mechanisms succeed or fail, but we continue to lack comparative cross-country empirical studies that examine the tangible outcomes produced by these institutions and the factors that explain these outcomes. Furthermore, there are no studies that compare the two models of participation identified here (radical participatory democracy and pragmatic citizen participation) in order to understand the characteristics that produce the most positive outcomes and the extent to which these models differ in practice.

ജ

In addition to engaging with the research questions posed in the introduction (what explains variation in outcomes between participatory mechanisms and to what extent the "radical" participatory democracy model provides more significant benefits than the more "pragmatic" experiments), this book addresses five related issues. First, we have seen that there remains a gap in the literature with respect to studies of concrete instances of popular participation. Despite the recent explosion of participatory mechanisms throughout Latin America, there has been relatively little comparative empirical research beyond the well-studied Brazilian participatory budgeting model. This gap is even more significant with respect to the "radical" participatory democracy innovations set up by governments in countries such as Venezuela and Ecuador, yet these institutions arguably come closest to the theoretical principles of participatory democracy. There is also a lack of comparative work that contrasts the two models of participation (radical participatory democracy and pragmatic citizen participation) in order to understand the characteristics that produce the most positive outcomes and the extent to which these models generate positive outcomes.

Second, there is an ongoing debate in the literature, the media, and the political arena with respect to factors that produce genuine democracy and the extent to which participatory institutions are able to generate more democratic outcomes. While the debate is not likely to be resolved due to different conceptions of democracy, it is necessary to engage in more empirical research that studies participatory institutions from a theoretically appropriate framework. Many who criticize participatory democracy use a normative interpretation that measures democratic innovations according to how far they diverge from the dominant Western model (Smilde 2011). These attacks are based on the very standards of the variant of democratic thought which the "radical" participatory initiatives seek to challenge. It is therefore no surprise that evaluations produced through this lens tend to be negative. Yet we have seen in this chapter that there is more than one conception of democracy and, while a given model may be less liberal, this does not automatically render it less democratic. Obviously, it is important to avoid the danger of stretching concepts to the extent that anything may be called "democracy" but at the same time, we must recognize that some initiatives that diverge from the dominant liberal conception may be more appropriate to a particular time and place. They must be assessed according to the vision of (participatory) democracy they are based on. Such an analysis should not preclude, of course, considering the concerns raised by opposing voices.

Third, if participatory institutions are able to produce some of the benefits identified in the theoretical literature, it is necessary to consider what characteristics of participatory mechanisms contribute to the achievement of meaningful outcomes. This should involve looking at both characteristics of the mechanisms themselves as well as how people use them (or attempt to use them) to achieve the outcomes they seek. Theorists have argued that certain characteristics must be in place in order for participatory institutions to be effective, yet as with the benefits themselves, these assertions have not been sufficiently tested. There has also been little attention to how citizens engage with participatory mechanisms beyond their formal characteristics. Comparing the outcomes and characteristics of different participatory institutions in different jurisdictions will provide insight on this important question.

Fourth, this book will engage critics of participatory mechanisms by asking to what extent they encourage citizenship as agency as their proponents argue, or citizenship as cooptation as their critics charge. In order to strengthen civil society by providing participants with real powers and encouraging citizenship as agency, participatory mechanisms must strike a delicate balance between autonomy and inclusion into political structures. If the latter is taken too far, it can lead to cooptation, yet without direct links to the state civil society will likely be excluded from decision making. We will look at how the radical vs. pragmatic models affect these factors.

Finally, we will study these questions from the perspective of the lived experiences of citizen participants who engage with participatory mechanisms on a daily basis. Much of the literature on democracy in Latin America suggests that what happens at the central level must infiltrate every level of the state, even down to local participatory mechanisms. Analyses of the state under "radical" leftist governments generally preclude the notion that different types of democratic practices may be occurring within the various institutions that make up the state. This creates a binary top-down vs. bottom-up dichotomy according to which authoritarian practices at the executive level negate the possibility that meaningful democratic practices are emerging at the local level. Understanding participatory democracy requires us to look beyond "big politics" and explore the "relational contexts in which politics occurs in everyday social life" (Smilde 2011). Political systems involve a number of contradictions and, in the case of participatory mechanisms, we must look at the local level in its own context and understand participatory processes through the experience of citizen participants.

Institutionalization of Citizen Participation in Venezuela, Ecuador, and Chile

Models of Participatory Design

We are taking a step forward, we are transcending a democracy that is merely representative and becomes a trap in which the aspirations of the people die and are buried . . . we are accelerating the construction of a participatory democracy, a Bolivarian democracy . . . a revolutionary democracy. The people are no longer the object but the subject. The people are taking the reins of the homeland.

—Hugo Chávez Frías, President of Venezuela (1999–2013), Aló Presidente no. 252, April 9, 2006

Democracy is perfectly compatible with a government that provides leadership and direction but that also benefits from an active citizenry that has the right to put forward ideas and possibilities. The idea is that the interaction between authorities and citizens will allow us to base public policy on the mutual responsibilities of these actors . . . public authorities responsible for governing with the people, and citizens in civil society responsible for contributing to a democratic government.

—Michelle Bachelet Jeria, President of Chile (2006–2010 and 2014–2018), Launch of the Pro-Participation Agenda, Santiago, September 29, 2006

These declarations, delivered by the presidents of two of the countries studied in this book, reveal some of the basic conceptual differences between "radical" participatory democracy and "pragmatic" citizen participation. In the discourse of the late Venezuelan leader, popular participation is framed not as being complementary to representative democracy but as an indispensable component of democracy itself. He distinguishes between "real" democracy and that which is "merely" formal and representative, suggesting that the political regimes of the past were illegitimate because the majority was excluded from the decision-making process. The solution, then, is to develop a new model in which the people play the role of protagonist, a "revolutionary" democracy according to Chávez. In contrast, Chilean President Michelle Bachelet frames participation more as a partnership between citizens and state institutions that should enhance good governance. She sees mutual benefit for citizens and authorities through increased public participation but does not seek to "revolutionize" democracy in any way.

Participatory mechanisms cannot be understood solely by examining how their respective states and their leaders frame participation nor can we only consider powers attributed to these institutions by enabling legislation. Rather, participatory mechanisms consist of three distinct elements that must be understood and evaluated: (1) The discourse through which they are promoted by politicians and state institutions, exemplified by the above quotations and materials produced by state agencies; (2) The institutional design of the mechanisms themselves; and (3) How they actually function in reality. This chapter will explore the first two by looking at the historical context of political participation and democracy in Venezuela, Ecuador, and Chile. It looks at state discourse behind the establishment of participatory mechanisms and describes the composition, attributions, and processes of the institutions studied in this book: communal councils (Venezuela), local citizens' assemblies (Ecuador), and neighborhood councils (Chile). The remainder of the book will focus on the third element: how the cases function in day-to-day life. We will see that while discourse, design, and reality may align, this is not always the case.

While there are differences between the models implemented in these countries, particularly with respect to the ideological framework, there are significant similarities that allow for meaningful comparisons. They are intended to make participation a regular part of peoples' lives as opposed to offering a temporary, "one shot" experience. Unlike citizens' juries and mini-publics that have emerged in Western contexts, they are not focused on a given policy area but territorially based and intended to cover a wide range of issues pertaining to local development. While they are legislated by the state in all three countries, the mechanisms are set up through citizens' own initiative. Residents of a given territory, rather than local authorities, are responsible for initiating and running their participatory mechanism. Also unlike most of the examples found in the North American and European literature, citizen participants are not selected to represent a given segment of the population; participation is open to everyone who resides within the given territory and anyone may participate at any time. In fact, particularly in the radical model, there is a deliberate intention not to simply reproduce representation within these new institutions but rather to encourage the community to engage.

Importantly for comparative purposes, the structure and powers of these mechanisms are established by national legislation. In most countries, including Brazil and Mexico, participatory institutions are set up by local levels of government in the absence of a national strategy. The existence of national enabling legislation makes between-country subnational comparisons more feasible, as we are essentially comparing three instances of institutional design. Comparisons with countries where institutions are implemented by various municipalities would introduce other variables related to different within-country institutional designs. Finally, while the powers devolved to these mechanisms differ among the three countries, all are formally integrated into the local policy process and have a legislated mandate to participate in local social and economic development, infrastructure, and neighborhood improvement. This allows for meaningful comparisons of participatory processes and outcomes.

There are also notable differences that must be acknowledged. In Venezuela and Ecuador, the discourse surrounding participation is similar: these states promote a conception premised on active, social, and collective citizenship that places primacy on direct participation in decision making (at the local level) in pursuit of communitarian goals. Citizens are not discussed as individuals but are conceived of in collective terms and organized into (state-sanctioned) participatory mechanisms. Venezuela's communal councils and Ecuador's local assemblies are part of a broader leftist agenda that promotes participation and are the result of constitutional renewal that seeks to institutionalize this agenda. In each case, the enabling legislation and subsequent government positions promote the values of radical participatory democracy that we find in the theoretical literature and an alternative model to "failed" representative democracy (see for example Universidad Bolivariana de Venezuela 2007; Consejo Federal de Gobierno 2008; Venezuela 2010; Ecuador 2010; SENPLADES 2011). These institutions and the broader framework they fit into (including the higher-level bodies they interface with) come closer than any other modern-day institutional arrangement to the theoretical models of radical democracy and bear striking similarities with the models proposed by theorists such as MacPherson (1977) and Barber (1984).

Chile's neighborhood councils are based on "pragmatic" or "instrumental" participatory democracy, according to which participation can strengthen the quality of democracy, provide more efficient services, and lead to more effective governance (see for example Ministerio Secretaría General de Gobierno 2012, 2013). This model seeks to strengthen representative democracy through citizen participation, not propose an alternative to it. The deliberation and decision-making processes are autonomous within the mechanisms themselves, but citizens must work with representative institutions and authorities make the final decisions during the implementation stage.

Emergence of Participatory Mechanisms

Venezuela: "Radical" Participatory Democracy

The period following the end of military rule (1958) is characterized as one of "pacted democracy" between a limited number of elite actors. Known as the Punto Fijo Pact, the agreement forged between Venezuela's two major political parties in 1958 created a highly unrepresentative system of two parties with a shared commitment to maintaining the status quo and excluding the popular sectors from decision making (Ellner 2008; Buxton 2009). It was this system—increasingly seen as illegitimate by the majority of Venezuelans—that Chávez successfully attacked through a "people's power" platform in the 1990s. While civil society in Venezuela has been historically weak, this began to evolve from the late 1980s onward, as citizens began to mobilize against the neoliberal austerity reforms imposed by the governments of Carlos Andrés Pérez (1989–1993) and Rafael Caldera (1994–1999). Popular neighborhoods of Caracas and other large urban centres witnessed the emergence of independent, grassroots neighborhood councils created as forums to discuss local needs and develop strategies for dealing with common problems in the absence of the state. These types of local popular initiatives grew from 1989 onward following the series of popular uprisings and state repression known as the *caracazo*.

With the ascension to power of Hugo Chávez, the concept of popular democracy was enshrined in the 1999 constitution as a first step in the "refounding" of the country's democracy.

The opening articles mention that the people's sovereignty must be exercised directly (article 5), but article 62 establishes a clearer definition of this "new" democracy. It states that "the participation of the people in the elaboration, implementation and control of public matters is necessary to guarantee their complete development as individuals and collectively." Constitutional language provides an important template for discourse related to citizenship and participation in Venezuela. The language used promotes active, participatory citizenship, with multiple references to solidarity, social equality, and communitarian values. Citizens are frequently described collectively as "el pueblo." This is a complex term which is generally understood to imply collective identity and is often represented in the singular, as a single virtuous entity that speaks with a united voice and seeks a "common good" (de la Torre 2010; Stehn 2011). The constitution also calls for the creation of institutions to channel this citizen participation, stating that communities will be incorporated into decision-making bodies that must be respected by authorities (article 70) (Venezuela 1999).

The first attempt to establish participatory mechanisms was launched in 2002, with the creation of Local Public Planning Councils (CLPPs). Based on participatory budgeting initiatives in Brazil, the CLPPs were intended to integrate popular participation into decision making at the municipal level, but participants complained that powerful local officials resisted citizen involvement. In April 2006, a new law formally established communal councils (*consejos comunales*) as a mechanism designed to address these issues through autonomy from local governments. The law reprises the language of participatory democracy and clearly establishes communal councils as the centerpiece of citizen participation in Venezuela (Venezuela 2006). Subsequent legislation, such as the 2009 reform of the Communal Council Law (which provides more power to these participatory mechanisms vis à vis local governments) and the 2010 People's Power Law, enforce the use of this discourse, describing citizens as playing the "leading role" in the democratic process, framing citizenship as communitarian and participation as revolutionary, collective, and aimed at achieving "the common good" (Venezuela 2009, 2010). One of the more interesting features of the reform is that it declares the communal councils to be a "public power" on the same footing as municipal, regional, and national governments.

The councils are thus meant to be the centrepiece of Venezuela's Bolivarian Revolution, a movement that, according to Chávez and supporters seeks to promote popular democracy, economic independence, and increased socioeconomic equality. Referring to the articles in the constitution, the enabling legislation describes them as "allowing the people to directly exercise management of public policy and projects related to their own needs" and as being "an important vehicle for the construction of a more equal society" (Venezuela 2006). They are intended to be autonomous bodies that have the power to make decisions about public matters, decisions that must be respected by elected authorities of the state. The councils have the power to establish and manage programs in local social and economic development, infrastructure, health, education, housing, sports, and other areas, and their decisions are not subordinated to the control of municipalities or other levels of government. The entire system of communal councils is under the oversight of a central government ministry, the *Ministerio del Poder Popular para las Comunas y los Movimientos Sociales* (MPComunas).

The participatory process is determined by the legislation and promoted through training materials developed by various central government agencies. Any citizen over the age of 15 can set up a communal council and no resources are required to do so. To set up a council, interested citizens must begin by calling a first meeting. If they are able to achieve quorum (10% of community members aged 15 and older), they can proceed to elect members and spokespeople who will establish the communal council. Any member of the community over 15 years of age is eligible to be elected to any council position or working group. Once the council is officially established (they must apply for and receive recognition from the central government, although legally this permission is only a formality if the members have proceeded according to the law), it must hold a meeting to assess community needs and to begin establishing priorities and considering how to obtain resources. While elected spokespeople drive the meeting agendas, all members of the council (the 200 to 400 families in an urban setting, for example) are eligible to participate in setting priorities and making decisions.

The councils are divided into a Citizens' Assembly comprised of all members of the represented community, an Executive consisting of elected spokespeople (*voceros*), as well as financial management, community oversight, and community engagement units, members of which are also elected by the Assembly. In addition to these organs, councils may elect to form work committees based on local needs (education, housing, electricity, sanitation, etc.) as well as cooperatives and even small businesses. Only the Assembly has the power to decide on matters and is able to exercise oversight of projects and budget.[1] Communal councils are expected to function according to an annual cycle which involves several phases known as the "Cycle of Communal Power": a "diagnostic" stage during which the council must engage in a participatory and deliberative process with the community to develop a needs assessment; a process of identifying the most pressing needs along with plausible solutions; the elaboration of the "Communal Development Plan," a funding phase, and an implementation phase.[2] The Assembly is supposed to be actively involved at all stages. Funding is complex: a portion of the national budget is allotted to funding communal council Development Plans but councils may also seek money from local governments and through fundraising or business activities. With respect to central government funding, proposed projects are evaluated and funding is attributed through a process that involves working groups made up of participants from various communal councils in a given territory working in collaboration with technical experts from agencies such as *Fundacomunal* and the *Consejo Federal de Gobierno* (a body charged with decentralization). In these *Salas de Batalla* (war rooms), delegates review all project submissions, categorize them into areas (health, infrastructure, etc.), and assign priorities based on the most pressing needs according to a defined methodology.[3]

In order to ensure popular input at higher levels of government in Venezuela, elected council spokespeople are able to participate in regional and national assemblies created for this purpose. A number of spokespeople from each council are elected to serve on the regional citizen assemblies, while delegates to the regional bodies are elected to serve on the national citizen assembly, chaired by the President of the Republic. Through these bodies, the councils are able to access and connect their communities' needs with other branches of government. Furthermore, the legislation is designed so that councils can form partnerships with each other to enhance their ability to move initiatives forward and also have links to other participatory institutions, such as local planning councils (Venezuela 2009; MPComunas, *El Poder popular*).

Training for those involved in participatory mechanisms is provided by numerous central and state government institutions including the *Servicio Autónomo Fondo Nacional de los Consejos Comunales* (SAFONACC) and the *Consejo federal de gobierno*. The regional offices deliver workshops and produce pedagogical materials on topics such as developing a budget, and/or writing project proposals and guidelines for community infrastructure projects.[4] The Ministry of Popular Power for Communes and Social Movements (MPComunas) and its regional offices also deliver workshops on participation more broadly (citizens' participatory rights, how various state institutions fit into the picture, etc.). Other state institutions provide more specific training. For example, the Central Bank of Venezuela provides workshops on topics such as "building the social economy."

Evidence suggests that the councils are popular among a large sector of the population. In 2008, only two years after their inception, 26,143 councils had been created in Venezuela, with another 10,669 in the process of being set up (FCG 2008). Considering that each council consists of 200 to 400 families, this translates into large numbers of people providing their insight and experience toward decision making on local matters. Survey data has been used to estimate that as many as 6 million adults, or about 35% of the eligible population, is or has been involved in a communal council (Hawkins 2010). They are thus arguably one of the most successful innovations of the "Bolivarian Revolution" led by Chávez's United Socialist Party of Venezuela (PSUV). However, critics charge that unlike the grassroots neighbourhood councils that emerged during the pre-Chávez period, the communal councils are state-generated institutions that seek to centralize and incorporate citizen participation into state-sanctioned forums (McCarthy 2012; Garcia-Gaudilla 2008).

Ecuador: Radical State Discourse, Limited Powers in Practice

While Ecuador made early strides toward decentralization throughout the 1980s and 1990s, popular participation has historically been limited and weak. Due to the decentralized nature of the political system, citizen participation has been extremely uneven and largely dependent on the willingness of provincial and municipal leaders. A number of experiments such as citizen' assemblies to provide input into budgeting were launched during this period, particularly in rural and small-town indigenous communities with varying results (Van Cott 2008). From the time of the establishment of liberal democracy (1979) through the late 2000s, however, citizens dissatisfied with government policies but excluded from any role in decision making tended to express themselves through extra-institutional tactics. During this period, Ecuador became one of the most politically unstable countries in the region as marginalized sectors (particularly indigenous peoples) with no access points to government developed some of the strongest social movement organizations in Latin America (Yashar 2005). Following the election of President Rafael Correa in 2007, popular participation has been promoted as part of a broader movement dubbed the Citizen's Revolution.

The new constitution, adopted in 2008 by referendum, declares that citizen participation in decision making is a fundamental right and states that citizens, as individuals or as part of a group, may exercise this right through various mechanisms (Ecuador 2008). The language used promotes active, participatory citizenship: references to "participation" and "partici-patory" appear even more frequently than in the Venezuelan *magna carta* and citizens are also frequently described collectively as "el pueblo." In 2010, the government followed up on these constitutional provisions with the adoption of the *Ley Orgánica de Participación Ciudadana* (Law of Citizen Participation). The law reaffirms participatory rights, using collective language to declare that all citizens and groups (such as indigenous nations) have the right to participate in decisions that involve them. It also creates the various types of mechanisms through which citizens may exercise these rights at every level of the state; an entire chapter of the law is dedicated to defining the composition and role of these state-sanctioned mechanisms. These include sectoral citizen councils corresponding to each government ministry and major policy area to promote dialogue, deliberation, and follow-up; citizen oversight bodies to provide "social control" and monitoring of policy implementation and public administration; participatory budgeting; and a *silla vacía* (empty seat) on local government bodies for one or more citizen representatives (Ecuador 2010b). The legislation requires agencies and departments at all levels of government (central, regional, provincial, and municipal) to establish a "system of citizen participation" which incorporates one or more of these mechanisms into planning and decision making. Legislation and other documents produced by the state claim that achieving this goal requires a redefinition and redesign of state institutions in order to move from a purely representative model to one that integrates citizens into the decision-making process and they prescribe and define a set of core participatory institutions through which citizens should ideally exercise these rights.[5] While the discourse that associates democracy with "the people" and popular participation is similar in many ways to that found in Venezuelan documents, the design of participatory mechanisms in Ecuador requires citizens to work with the state and local authorities through participatory mechanisms. The state planning agency (SENPLADES) affirms that participatory planning makes citizens and the state "jointly responsible for the design and management of public policy and action."[6]

Of all the newly created institutions, those that most closely resemble Venezuela's communal council model are the local citizen assemblies (*asambleas ciudadanas locales*). Citizens can form an assembly at their own initiative and once established they can put forward development plans and local policy initiatives, administer service and infrastructure improvements, promote education with respect to citizen rights, and exercise oversight over decisions made (Ecuador 2010, articles 56–60). A founding group of citizens must first elicit interest among fellow citizens, convene a meeting of those interested in forming an assembly, and elect spokespeople to guide the institution. The process they are expected to follow mirrors that of Venezuelan communal councils: needs assessment (diagnostic); prioritization and budgeting (in collaboration with municipal and regional-level participatory mechanisms convened by the corresponding level of government); the elaboration of a Development Plan, implementation of selected projects (described as "participatory management"), and an evaluation stage which involves citizen oversight and accountability to the local assemblies involved in the project.[7] While participatory, the process demonstrates more involvement from elected officials and civil servants than in Venezuela, and decisions about funding are made in fora that include both citizen and local government representatives. A senior official charged with implementing participatory democracy described a process which involves three sets of actors: citizens, local authorities, and representatives from the appropriate government department. Citizen participation occurs when these three are able to work together; citizen involvement lends legitimacy to the process.[8]

As in Venezuela, the local assemblies can "feed up" by sending representatives to provincial and regional assemblies and there are seats reserved for local assembly representatives on other participatory bodies, such as National Planning Council and relevant sectoral councils. Oversight for the entire system of popular participation is provided by a central government ministry, the *Secretaría Nacional de Gestión de la Política*, which is charged with ensuring that central and local government departments fulfil their obligations. The *Consejo de Participación Ciudadana y Control Social* (CPCCS) serves as the interface between the central government and the various participatory institutions created by the Citizen Participation Law. The body is itself made up of citizens elected to serve for a set term and employs a number of technicians charged with supporting citizens involved in the various participatory mechanisms. Training is provided by these two agencies as well. The CPCCS, for example, has a participation "advisor" (*asesor/a*) for each province who is dedicated to travel to various communities to promote participatory rights and deliver training and has also developed an online course for citizen participation.

Given that the Ecuadorian process is relatively new, these efforts have tended to focus on teaching relevant legislation and guiding people with respect to how to set up citizen assemblies.[9] As in Venezuela, instruction provided by Ecuadorian institutions charged with supporting citizen participation promotes active participatory citizenship which includes sectors traditionally excluded in decisions that affect their lives, while simultaneously limiting this participation to certain domains and mechanisms and incorporating it into the state. While promoting the idea of a profound democratic reform of the state, there is more of a focus on co-management, with the people defined as playing a leading role, yet in cooperation with state actors.[10] The mechanics of participation, then, appear to deviate somewhat from the overreaching "citizens' revolution" discourse in that "people's power" gives legitimacy to, rather than replaces, representatives. While the higher-level discourse is framed as "radical" democracy in terms of citizen autonomy and devolution of powers, the day-to-day working of participatory mechanisms looks more like the Chilean model.

Chile, Pragmatic Citizen Participation

Since Chile's return to democracy in 1990, the country has regularly been considered a model of representative democracy in the region but one of the least participatory political systems. The country's constitution, promulgated under the Pinochet regime and modified numerous times since 1990, does not establish citizen participation as a right. Discourse found in the Chilean constitution is quite distinct from the other two countries. There are few references to "participation" and citizenship is strikingly absent from the Chilean constitution other than as they relate to a legal status, with various sets of political and civil (but not social) rights.

Despite this context, Chile was in fact one of the first countries in Latin America to establish a system of participatory mechanisms through national legislation. The *juntas de vecinos* (neighborhood councils) have a history rooted in a particular conception of participatory democracy.

Created in 1968, the councils were the centerpiece of the Popular Promotion program of the government of President Eduardo Frei (1964–1970)
aimed at reducing marginality. Frei's Christian Democrats identified the
low living standards of Chile's poor as tied to lack of political participation
and sought to develop institutions that would allow people to participate
in addressing their own problems (Oxhorn 1995). The *juntas* lost much of
their independence during the Pinochet dictatorship, but regained some
vitality in the 1990s. Oxhorn (1995) observes that in the years following
the return to democracy, the roles and activities of these institutions
were expanding and they demonstrated great potential, particularly with
respect to neighborhood improvement and standard of living issues. Still,
the concern of the successive *Concertación* governments (1990–2010)
with containing popular mobilization meant that the capacity of these
mechanisms as an agent of large-scale participation remained limited.
A 1997 law more clearly defines the functions of the councils, which
include proposing and managing projects that benefit the neighborhood
and addressing common problems and development issues in conjunction
with local authorities (Chile 1997). The establishment of a council is at
the initiative of community members, who must gather the necessary
number of participants (50 for a commune of less than 10,000 residents)
and have their council recognized by the municipal authorities.[11] Through
the neighborhood councils, citizens are able to obtain improvements
to their neighborhoods, although they need to work through state and
local government departments because these councils do not have actual
decision-making powers.

The process that neighborhood councils must follow to propose and
implement projects is far less defined than in the other two countries.
There are no established guides, processes, and methodologies. Rather,
council leaders (*dirigentes*) generally establish lists of priorities based on
feedback from regular contact with their neighbours. They then convoke
an assembly which everyone in the areas represented by the council may
attend, present their list, and ask neighbours to vote on the projects they
wish the council to pursue. Once a list of priorities is established, the
dirigentes must then attempt to convince local officials (either mayors,
municipal councillors, or relevant bureaucrats) that the project has the
support of the community and should be funded and implemented. Unlike
in the Venezuelan case, funding decisions are at the discretion of elected
officials or civil servants and implementation is generally managed by state
agencies, with "oversight" from neighborhood councils.[12]

Despite a notable lack of popular participation in the Chilean context, the theme emerged as part of the political discourse under the first administration of President Michelle Bachelet (2006–2010) and continued under the administration of her predecessor, Sebastián Piñera (2010–2014), resulting in the adoption of a Citizen Participation Law (2011) that establishes participation as a right and creates new participatory institutions at all levels of government, including Civil Society Councils intended to enhance participation at the municipal level by providing a forum for civil society actors (including neighborhood councils) to interact with elected officials. The law also recognizes the neighborhood councils as legal entities and creates a new source of funding for projects promoted by the councils. While the effectiveness of the neighborhood councils had long been criticized because of the lack of formal linkages between local councils (leading to fragmentation of demands), the 2011 law allows them to form unions comprised of representatives from various councils within the same commune. They can use these unions to address common concerns and to pool their resources, a strategy which should in theory give participants greater power vis à vis local governments.

Unlike in the other two cases, the discourse used in the new legislation does not employ the language of "people's power" or suggest that some kind of revolution in the relationship between "el pueblo" (a term which is not used) and the state is taking place. Rather, it tends to frame citizens' participation in practical and pragmatic terms, emphasizing "more effective and efficient" public policy, "strengthening communication between citizens and the government," and "increasing transparency and confidence" in government institutions. The law clearly establishes citizen participation as falling "within a framework of co-responsibility" between citizens and the state and participation is primarily consultative; there is no sense that the people play a direct leading role in decision making.[13]

Training for participation is less common than in Venezuela and Ecuador. When provided, training is usually offered by the department of the municipal (commune) government responsible for enacting citizen participation initiatives, although the new legislative framework establishes a School of Public Management for leaders of social organizations (including neighborhood councils). The relative lack of formal training is not surprising given that much of the work central to the participatory process in Venezuela and Ecuador (diagnostic, elaboration of development plans and budgets, etc.) is carried out by municipal and other state agencies in the Chilean context. Certain central government ministries, including the

Secretaría de Gobierno, play a significant role in promoting the state's new policy on public participation and a growing number of municipalities are creating departments charged with promoting and supporting citizen participatory initiatives, although the process is quite uneven (Marín and Mlynarz, 2012). In the Chilean context then, it is difficult to separate participation from co-responsibility and co-management.

We have seen what participatory mechanisms are supposed to do according to the governments that designed and implemented these initiatives. The next three chapters will look at how they work in practice.

PART II

THE CASES

This book engages with the questions posed in the previous chapters by looking at a particular type of participatory innovation that has emerged across Latin America: local citizens' councils that provide individuals with the opportunity to engage in the decision-making process at the neighborhood level in an institutionalized environment. These mechanisms (called communal councils in Venezuela, local citizens' assemblies in Ecuador, and neighborhood councils in Chile) share a number of characteristics that facilitate such comparisons and distinguish them from some of the experiments Western observers are familiar with. They are all local (generally neighborhood-level) mechanisms intended to make participation a regular part of peoples' lives and cover a wide range of issues pertaining to local development. They are established and regulated by national legislation but residents of a given territory, rather than local authorities, are responsible for initiating and running them. Citizen participants are not selected to represent a given segment of the population: participation is open to everyone who resides within the given territory. They generally consist of a directive made up of elected volunteers and a citizens' assembly—which all residents may attend—that has final decision-making authority. Internal procedures tend to value deliberation over voting and aggregation of interests, particularly in the radical model.

There are also notable differences that will be explored throughout this book. Pragmatic citizen participation seeks to enhance rather than replace representation and provides better governance through citizen involvement in decision making while radical participatory democracy claims to challenge dominant Western conceptions by integrating "the people" (*el pueblo*) into the policy process, at least at the local level.

Mechanisms based on radical participatory democracy principles are characterized by a greater devolution of powers to citizens at the local level (at least on paper). They meet many of the criteria of participatory democracy theory and thus have the potential to produce significant outcomes, but the politicized nature and polarization of the environments in which they emerge may make them susceptible to controlled inclusion. Pragmatic citizen participation mechanisms do not have the same formal powers and are not backed by a "power to the people" discourse. They play more of a limited consultative role, but their less politicized and polarized nature should insulate them from political interference. These differences are not only discursive and ideological but also translate into variation on a number of factors, including formal powers and relationships with government authorities.

Evaluation of Outcomes

Evaluating the impact of participatory programs and mechanisms remains notoriously difficult (Nabatchi, 2012; Burton, 2009; Rowe and Frewer 2000). There are no agreed-upon methods for assessing the outcomes of citizen participation, and it is understood that measurement of outcomes is particularly complex (Abelson and Gauvin 2006). Institutional design and goals vary considerably, making it difficult to deploy a single rigorous assessment tool across all cases. It is often not clear what constitutes a "good" or significant outcome, and there are obviously difficulties with respect to establishing causal links between participatory processes and concrete outcomes.

In the absence of an established framework, there are a number of criteria we can use to assess participatory experiences (see table 4.1). First, the scope of the outcomes is an important factor to consider. Do the outcomes affect large numbers of people in the jurisdiction represented by a given participatory mechanism, or do they benefit only a few (Burton, 2009)? Were significant quantities of resources deployed as a result of participation? Comparisons between the cases help to determine the scope. Second, while determining what constitutes a "significant" outcome will remain ambiguous, it is possible to study whether the outcomes align with the decisions made by citizens through their participatory process. Third, in the context of developing countries we can look for evidence that outcomes have improved the standard of living or material conditions of a significant proportion of the population represented by the participatory mechanism. Based on these criteria, outcomes produced by the participatory mechanisms can be ranked as high, medium, low, or of no value. To be clear, the purpose of this book is not to conduct a formal program review of the outcomes of each mechanism but rather to establish some assessable criteria for comparative purposes.

One of the novel features of this book is to tell the story of participatory mechanisms from the perspective of participants. In order to rank the outcomes according to these criteria, we will utilize the interview data to consider their perspectives with respect to alignment and material conditions. These perspectives are supported and enhanced by drawing on interviews with various public officials involved in the participatory processes and by documentation produced by the participatory mechanisms and relevant local and national government agencies.

Table 4.1. Evaluation Criteria, Tangible Outcomes[1]

	Alignment	Scope	Material Conditions
High Value	Outcomes are directly aligned with decisions made through participation	Outcomes are significant in scope and affect a significant proportion of the given population	Significant improvement to peoples' standard of living
Medium Value	Outcomes are mostly aligned with decisions made through participation	Outcomes are moderate in scope and affect a fair proportion of the given population	Modest improvement to peoples' standard of living
Low Value	Some alignment with decisions made through participation	Outcomes are minor in scope and affect a small proportion of the given population	Little improvement to peoples' standard of living
No Value	No alignment with decisions made through participation	No demonstrable outcomes or outcomes affect only a select few	No improvement to peoples' standard of living

1. Adapted from Burton, 2009.

4

Venezuela

Radical Participatory Democracy

Venezuela can be considered the prototype for the radical model of participatory democracy in Latin America. State discourse behind the creation and development of communal councils promotes a profound break with the past. These mechanisms are touted as the centerpiece of a new model of democracy that will change the power relationship between marginalized sectors and traditional local authorities. Their institutional design goes further than perhaps any other participatory innovations in the region and aligns with the criteria put forward in the theoretical literature on public participation. But are they actually having an impact on people's quality of life and on how people feel about their role as citizens or is all of this simply a façade (or worse, a means of incorporating popular participation into the state)? To what extent do they encourage citizenship as agency as their proponents argue, or citizenship as cooptation as their critics charge? What characteristics of the mechanisms explain these outcomes?

Venezuela's communal councils perform well in terms of both tangible and "soft" outcomes, with some variation between the three cases. The cases studied in this chapter have been successful with respect to achieving significant improvements to the neighborhoods they represent. These benefits have been achieved in a timely manner and are closely aligned with the needs that members identified. The cases demonstrate a real devolution of decision making to citizens, they allow for bottom-up political participation and deliberation (as opposed to being merely consultative), they are inclusive in that participation has been expanded to traditionally disadvantaged groups, and decisions made through this process can be translated into action. They also enjoy a relatively high level of participation and commitment and a strong culture of social organization. Yet we also see evidence of the dangers that state-sanctioned participatory mechanisms such as communal councils can present in a highly polarized political environment. In Venezuela, both the design of these institutions and state discourse surrounding citizens' power create relationships with the state that promote more inclusive decision making while establishing parameters around democratic participation. This may threaten to tip the delicate "inclusion-cooptation balance" toward controlled inclusion.

The chapter begins with an introduction to the cases. It then discusses the outcomes they have achieved, the characteristics of these mechanisms that help to explain these outcomes, state-society relations, and the weaknesses and potential dangers of the Venezuelan model.

The Cases

The first case is located in the Catia district of Sucre Parish on the west side of Caracas. The parish is primarily working-class and is representative of the Capital District in that it falls in the middle of the spectrum with respect to various socioeconomic indicators, including inadequate housing (3% of households in 2011, down from 5.7% in 2001) and lack of basic services (1.5%, down from 2.6%). It is strongly *chavista* and its residents are also well known for playing a central role in social and political events, such as the mass demonstrations that returned Chávez to power after a failed coup attempt in 2002. The parish is the home of important community-based organizations such as Catia TV, a television station managed by individuals from the parish's various social organizations (including local communal councils). The council represents about 350 families and has 126 active members. A majority of respondents (56%) were women and 81% were above the age of 40. The largest number of respondents (26%) identified themselves as unskilled laborers (generally in the informal sector). This category includes many construction workers and self-employed individuals. Other common categories include homemakers, domestic workers, educators, skilled tradespeople, and retired people. An overwhelming 92% professed support for then-President Chávez and his party. The area represented by the council is a working-class district of mid-to-high-density housing (apartment blocks built during the 1950s and 1960s) and small businesses located near the parish's main artery. The communal council itself operates out of its own building purchased with funds earmarked for this purpose; it contains meeting rooms and space for community events. The surrounding area suffers from older, eroding infrastructure, particularly with respect to sewage and water, and many of the residential buildings have deteriorated over the years, particularly the roofing.

The second case is situated in Yagua, Municipality of Guacara in Carabobo (Central Region). With just over 24,000 residents, Yagua has a small population but is spread out over a relatively large area. In 2011, about 15% of the population was considered poor, while 2.8% lived in extreme poverty, down considerably from 31% and 6.6% in 2001.[1] Yagua is primarily rural but has gradually been developing due to the encroaching urban sprawl of Greater Valencia, Venezuela's third largest city. Many of the homes are detached with small parcels of land and most are relatively recent, having been built within the last 15 years but are in varying states of repair. Because the area was settled relatively recently, infrastructure is not fully developed. Many residents still lack reliable basic services (particularly electrical), many streets remain unpaved (and become muddy in the rainy season) and some of the houses constructed with the aid of Misión Vivienda are already beginning to deteriorate in Carabobo's humid climate.[2] Securing adequate housing for residents who have acquired land through land invasions or redistribution programs has been one of the primary objectives of the council. Unlike the Catia case, the communal council does not operate out of its own building but rather out of the local elementary school (several members of the council are teachers at the school). It represents about 213 families and has 49 active members. Many of these families acquired their property through land occupations and land redistribution programs initiated by the Chávez government. The largest number of respondents (21%) identified themselves as informal laborers. Other common categories include homemakers, agricultural workers, teachers, formal laborers, skilled tradespeople, and small farmers. A strong majority (83%) identified as pro-Chávez.

The third case is located in Belén, a sector in central Mérida, a mid-sized city in the Andean region. Capital of the state of the same name, Mérida is home to one of Venezuela's most important universities (the Universidad de los Andes) and has recently become a stronghold of support for opposition candidates and political movements. Belén is a quiet, leafy residential area within walking distance of the city's colonial main square. It is characterized primarily by semi-detached, single-family dwellings, interspersed with small business (shops, restaurants, etc.) and small plazas and parks. While the neighborhood was settled in the early to mid-20th century, infrastructure has been relatively well maintained and most homes are in a good state of repair. While many of the homes need to replace their roofing (and this has been an important goal of the council), many of the projects have been focused on community improvement, such as the construction of a sports court and a kitchen for the local school. This contrasts somewhat with the first two cases, in which councils were more concerned with basic infrastructure and housing improvement projects. The communal council operates out of peoples' homes; active members tend to meet and work in each other's residences on a rotating basis, while assembly meetings are either held in a plaza or at the local school sports arena. It represents 234 families and has about 48 active members. In terms of occupations, there is more variety here than in the other two cases, with a higher number of individuals who can be classified as professionals. A number of individuals were employed in tourism, Mérida having long established itself as a tourist center in the Venezuelan Andes. Whereas in the other two cases, council leaders tended to identify their members as "poor," "working-class," or "humble," the spokespeople for this council were keen to point out that most participants should be considered middle-class.

Outcomes

All three of these communities have experienced concrete benefits in the form of infrastructure modernization, housing improvements, and other social development programs intended to augment residents' quality of life. In all cases, residents, local officials, and available documentation link these gains to the communal councils, and individuals interviewed almost unanimously feel that such benefits are more equitably distributed than in the past. Respondents agreed that their quality of life and access to public goods and services, which they see as democratic rights, have improved as a result of the direct participation of their community in decision making and project implementation. Communities are using these institutions to resolve long-standing infrastructure problems (access to treated water and sewage and electricity, among others) that municipal governments prior to the establishment of councils tended to ignore. Activists who claim that municipal and regional governments of the past only devoted resources to middle-class and wealthy neighborhoods believe that the communal councils have allowed inhabitants of poorer *barrios* and rural areas access to public goods they were denied in the past. There is some variation between the cases, however, particularly with respect to the council located in Belén (Mérida) which has thus far produced medium-value outcomes, although needs identified were less acute and smaller in scope (see table 4.2).

Catia

This case exhibits the most significant outcomes of the cases studied in terms of the scope of the projects and number of residents affected, alignment with participants' wishes, and amelioration of material conditions. The alternatives identified by residents through the council's assembly are focused on improving the infrastructure in the neighborhood, which suffers from deteriorating sewage and housing conditions. Improving the state of housing complexes was also deemed to be a concern in this high-density sector of Caracas.[3]

Residents were particularly keen to point out the more equitable access to public goods and services they had witnessed since the creation of their communal council. Nere, a retail worker and council participant, explained what many of her neighbors expressed:

Table 4.2. Outcome Evaluation Criteria, Venezuela

Case	Tangible Outcomes	Alignment with Alternatives	Scope	Improvement to Quality of Life	Participants' Role in Participatory Relationship	Participants' Role Aligns with Institutional Design
Catia	High Value	*Strong*	*Large*	*Significant*	Dominant	Yes
Yagua	High Value	*Strong*	*Large*	*Significant*	Dominant	Yes
Belém	Medium Value	*Strong-Moderate*	*Moderate*	*Moderate*	Mostly dominant	Mostly

It used to be that decisions were made only by a few people in our municipalities. These tended to be people with more money and contacts, projects went to neighborhoods where these people and their friends lived. Now, you don't have to be from one of these families to participate in decisions about your own neighbourhood.[4]

An early initiative undertaken involved the reconstruction of drainage and sewage systems for the neighborhood blocks represented by the council. The project was carried out over the next two years and resulted in laying down over 800 meters of new pipes, repairing an additional 1,200 meters, and improving access to and from the system to buildings covering 11 blocks.[5] About 200 families, or over 800 people, benefited (over 40% of residents in the neighborhood represented by the council). The project plan provides a detailed timeline for completion, an extensive list of materials required (from tools to pipes to concrete), calculations and diagrams depicting the area to be updated, a detailed budget, and the number of laborers required. As per the communal council's decision, a stipulation was included ensuring that workers from the area represented by the council be given priority and that materials would also be purchased from local business whenever possible. This provided temporary employment to 40 individuals.

The project was decided on in a near-unanimous vote at one of the council's earliest assemblies in 2007 and was then developed into a detailed plan that was submitted to Fundacomunal and FIDES[6] for funding later that year. The project was deemed essential in the council's proposal due to "significant structural deterioration of the sewer network" which was identified as the most significant problem facing this popular sector as residents have been seriously affected by sewage waters running through some streets, which causes infection, illness, and general unpleasantness due to the noxious odors.[7] While the sewage system had not deteriorated across the entire neighborhood represented by the council, the proposal insists that the quality of life of all residents has been affected and that even those whose homes were not directly touched voted to make this a priority at the council's assembly meeting. A working committee of local residents was elected to take the lead on the project and report back to the assembly. Local officials responsible for funding and technical support to communal councils pointed to this as an example of how these participatory mechanisms should work, arguing that they encourage solidarity, community values, and deliberation. These qualities, along with the demonstration of need, are the factors used to determine funding for this and other projects.[8] While technicians from the Technical Support System for Communal Councils (SINATECC) provided necessary technical support, the council's elected *voceros* and relevant working committee members were involved at all stages of the project, from developing the proposal to presenting the plan and making the case for funding at the parish's annual *Sala de Batalla* (war room, the process during which various councils present their projects for funding) to the implementation stage. Javi, a shoe salesman and former *vocero*, expressed a sentiment typical of how many of his neighbors felt:

> Do you know how bad it was with the drainage system before? It was unhealthy for us, the city hadn't fixed it for decades. Do you think the government back then cared or did anything? No, we tried to deal with it but they didn't listen, they weren't working for us. With the communal council, with participation, we work for ourselves, we decide what we are going to do here. So we decided to fix the drainage ourselves.[9]

Another major project, the improvement of the district's water system, was undertaken in 2009. The communal council's involvement included purchasing the materials, managing the budget, and hiring local labor (approximately 20 local workers were hired).[10] A total of 238 families benefited. This project was identified as the most pressing need in 2009 due to health concerns surrounding drinking water. Members of the executive, working groups, and representatives of families living in the buildings targeted for water system improvements were involved at all stages of the process, including implementation and evaluation. Participants felt that the needs were pressing enough to ensure that all members were inclined to support these projects whether or not their families were directly affected. Martin, a shop attendant, stressed the role of his neighbors in deciding priorities:

> The community was waiting for years for funding to upgrade this infrastructure but it never came, in part because of corruption under the old system, local politicians would just steal

the money and what could the people do? Now, they can't do that because the community gets to decide, so we finally got the water system and drains fixed.[11]

Residents were also involved in a major project aimed at improvements to housing in the area, particularly roofing. This initiative resulted in repairs to 30 housing complexes and semi-detached homes, benefiting over 450 families. The council has since voted to establish this as an annual program, with the process beginning at the start of each "communal power cycle."[12] As with the other two projects, materials were purchased locally when possible and residents from the neighborhood were hired to do the work. Given that the housing improvement project was intended to benefit particular dwellings as opposed to entire blocks, the decision-making process was considerably more complicated. Still, participants and local officials involved in funding and technical support agree that the process was democratic and worked according to the principles of "communitarian democracy." Residents were asked to nominate families whose homes they believed were in dire need of structural repairs and a council working group was established to inspect these homes and establish a "greatest needs" list. Two members of a communal council located in another parish were brought in and asked to report on incidents of bias or corruption. While there was some dissent with respect to the homes selected, the individuals interviewed agreed that the process was fair, with most arguing that it was considerably more democratic and transparent than the "old way," in which municipal officials made these kinds of decisions. Typical of the responses provided by participants, Iris, a homemaker, recalled:

> I remember years ago, every house in this neighbourhood was falling apart, our roofs were leaking a lot. Nobody did anything about it, nobody cared, it was up to us to fix it they said. But how could we make expensive repairs with the salaries they want to pay us? Now . . . every roof on this street has been repaired in the last five years and on top of that, we were able to take charge of this ourselves through our communal council.[13]

The initiatives discussed above represent the major projects completed, but a number of minor initiatives were also undertaken, including repairs to the council's headquarters and purchasing various materials (books, art supplies, etc.) for the local elementary school. The council's executive also considered creating and funding a "security" force, as other councils in Sucre parish have done, in response to rising crime problems. However, the citizens' assembly rejected this proposal, with opponents arguing successfully that arming more local citizens was not an ideal use of funds. Instead, the assembly decided that the council should work on forging better relationships with the local division of the Bolivarian National Police.[14] More recently, residents voted in favor of an initiative that will establish programs for teenagers aimed at keeping them "out of trouble." This includes sports and job skills programs.

Yagua

Members of this council were extremely consistent with respect to identifying the most significant problems facing their community. Because the area was settled relatively recently, infrastructure is not fully developed. Many residents still lack reliable basic services (particularly electrical), many streets remain unpaved (and become muddy in the rainy season) and many of the houses are in poor condition. The lack of paved roads creates sanitary and transportation/access problems, particularly as many residents are required to trudge through mud to get to and from home. Many of the homes that have been built remain off the power grid and have no access to sewage and plumbing. Building adequate housing for residents who have acquired land through land invasions or redistribution programs has been one of the primary objectives of the council. Residents voted to make these problems a priority and the council has been quite successful in achieving these goals through its participatory planning and budgeting process.[15] Obtaining titles to the land that families' homes are built on has been another important component of the council's housing policy agenda.

Between 2010 and 2012, 50 homes were built on lots in the area and the council was in the process of building 30 more at the time of this research. Over 250 people in the semi-rural community have benefited from the project directly through new housing, while over 20 local workers have been employed in the construction of the homes during this same time period.[16] The homes were built with quality materials and designed to be weather resistant, but lacked services such as electricity and plumbing, although septic tanks were installed to deal with sewage as this was considered the minimum required for a "dignified" quality of life. The lack of adequate housing was deemed a priority from the time the council began operating in 2007. The first elected executive council established a working committee to tackle the issue and a proposal was subsequently brought forward to the citizen's assembly that provided a detailed plan for building 50 homes over the next two years. The proposal argued that housing is "a basic necessity for members of our community and for all citizens in order to live in a dignified manner" and that making this a priority over all other community objectives was in line with the ideas of "21st Century Socialism" and with communitarian values. There was considerable discussion over the proposal (in which families without adequate housing participated) and it was adopted by a unanimous assembly vote. The actual project, developed by the council in collaboration with Misión Vivienda, included participant input regarding the materials to be used and a detailed timeline (from purchasing the materials and preparing the lots to painting the finished houses).[17] Families that moved into the new homes were extremely pleased with both the houses and the process. As Geraldina, a domestic worker who moved to the area from a poorer region on the coast explained:

> A roof over your head isn't just something that is nice to have, it is a human right. Before, us poor people had to use most of our earnings just to put a substandard roof over our heads . . . And now we can be involved in decisions about these kinds of things, I mean I was involved in the planning and construction of my own home.[18]

Extending electricity and sewage to newly constructed homes is part of the second phase of the council's social development plan. Given that newly built homes lack all basic services, residents were required to choose between a set of services they wished to have access to. Electrification was selected as a priority because it was considered more feasible to provide power lines than to extend the sewage and water systems, an initiative which would have cost more. The council executive put forward a proposal (adopted by the assembly) that focused on ensuring that homes without electricity would be connected to the grid within a year and that septic tanks would be installed in newly built homes without access to sewage. Council participants from various parts of neighborhood conducted a census in order to determine which homes needed these services. The council received funding from both Fundacomunal and the municipality of Guacara through processes that included representatives from various communal councils.

According to members of the executive council and confirmed by a municipal official, 100 homes in a 1.8 sq. kilometer area were provided with electricity by extending the grid from sections of the parish closest to the area without service. This was followed by the purchase and installation of septic tanks for the new homes (up to 80) over the following year. While the electrical service is provided by the state-owned National Electric Corporation (Corpoelec), the communal council has the authority to "coordinate" the service in collaboration with Corpolec representatives and municipal officials. This involved supervision of the installation of the service as well as ongoing coordination of service provision, performance, and maintenance. In order to take on this role, the council established an electrification committee with representatives from the target community. This "round table" works with the newly established Institute for Community Technical Training, a body set up by the mayor of Guacara to provide technical assistance to members of the municipality's communal councils.

Residents feel that having the communal council involved in provision of basic services allows for a higher degree of responsiveness, as explained by Anita, a school kitchen worker whose home was electrified in 2008:

> I have electricity in my home thanks to the communal council. Yes, there are blackouts but my neighbours are part of the *mesa* (electrification round table) and they have the power to do something when there are problems, so it isn't like calling a big bureaucracy that doesn't care. Through the council we can exercise control over these things that affect our lives.[19]

From 2008 to 2012, about 50 streets in the area represented by the council have been paved. This has benefited over 400 families and has improved their quality of life by creating a cleaner environment and making transportation more accessible.[20] As with the other projects, local workers were hired to do the work and materials were purchased from local businesses when possible. Streets to be paved were chosen in a participatory process, but selection was made according to certain criteria also discussed and debated by the council's citizens' assembly. Unpaved streets with the greatest number of homes were identified in order to ensure that the largest number of residents benefited. Also, while not every residential street could be paved immediately, arteries that connect with major paved roads were identified to ensure that at least every home would be within a couple of blocks from a paved street. As with the other projects, the process ensured that unemployed residents would have priority in being hired as laborers and materials would be purchased from local sources when possible. Citizens were generally quite satisfied with these outcomes, often comparing them to past experiences, as Maria S., a council participant, explains:

> I've lived here for 15 years and during most of that time our streets weren't paved so we had to deal with dirt in the dry season and mud in the rainy season, And back then the city, governments only paved certain parts of the cities, and which parts do you think they paved? The parts where people with more money lived, of course, not here, not where people like us live. But now we don't have to worry about them (elected officials) because we have the communal council, so we can participate and things can get done for everyone, even the poor.[21]

Residents have also been working on gaining the legal status required to manage the district's water supply. Maricruz, a council member charged with pursuing this goal argued that "democratization also involves giving ownership of natural resources to the people who use them. Water is not a commodity it belongs to the community, it used to be in the hands of a private company but our members want to manage these resources themselves and the council has mechanisms to ensure they are being used well."[22] Another important initiative has been to assist residents in obtaining titles for the land they occupy. As mentioned, many locals inhabit land acquired through occupations or redistribution programs but this land legally belongs to the National Land Institute (INTI), a state agency charged with administering land redistribution. While they cannot own the land (it remains in the hands of the state), they may obtain titles that allow them to legally occupy it, use it for production, and pass the land on to their heirs. Because the process is complex, the council has set up a working group of citizens who have been trained to assist residents in obtaining these titles; more than 70 families have benefited so far.

Citizen participants indicated a strong satisfaction with these out-comes and with the participatory process through the communal council, arguing that the benefits were a result of their own work, or that they were actively involved in various stages of the process. Municipal officials agreed that these outcomes are the result of the communal council's work and insist that the municipality only provided the necessary technical support.

Belén

The neighborhood represented by this communal council is located in an established middle-income part of Mérida. The needs identified were decidedly different and this is reflected in the alternatives that residents chose to pursue and the relatively limited scope of the outcomes. While they do align to an extent with the alternatives identified by participants, there are some gaps where projects had not yet been implemented a year after decisions were made by the council's assembly. There is also more disagreement among participants with respect to the quality of the outcomes. Some local citizens indicated a strong satisfaction and believed that the community's standard of living had improved when compared with the period prior to the existence of the communal council. Others were less pleased, with several participants expressing dissatisfaction with the politicized nature of the council, arguing that benefits are sometimes distributed unequally, with known *chavistas* more likely to be favored.

The projects tackled by the communal council include improvements to neighborhood facilities as opposed to large-scale infrastructure projects. These were selected among the alternatives presented at the council's assembly.[23] The first involved revamping the local sports center. The court was remodeled and modernized with a new roof and facilities, and new sports equipment was purchased. This was deemed to be an important benefit for local children and teenagers. Residents identified the neighborhood sports facility as a priority through the citizens' assembly as it provides not only a physical place for young people to go but activities to keep them "out of trouble." The council's financial organ held a competition to select people to work on the project and purchase materials, while a separate elected working group was established to carry it forward and report back to the assembly. Again, the council accepted proposals from local groups of workers and chose what they considered to be the best proposal. Another project was the construction of a dining facility (including a kitchen) for the local school. The school, which welcomes primarily underprivileged children from the neighborhood represented by the council and from other sectors of the city, lacked such facilities and this was used as the justification for this project. The dining room was built and furnished with kitchen equipment; state funding ensures that children receive free meals. It is estimated that over 200 underprivileged children have benefited from these facilities.[24] Many respondents provided even more specific examples of concrete benefits, often referring to their children as well. Some stressed that programs and services that may seem inconsequential to "the elites" are important benefits for the poor. As one mother explained:

> The school provides two meals for our kids: breakfast and lunch. They provide milk and healthy meals. This is no small thing for us, this takes a big burden off us parents because we want our kids to be well fed but it is costly. It is a relief to send my children to school and know they will eat.[25]

Members also elected to pursue a scholarship program that provides grants to young people in the represented area. At the time of this research, about 20 individuals had benefited from this program, many of whom are studying at the nearby Universidad de los Andes (ULA). Selection of eligible beneficiaries is made by the council's education committee, whose members are elected by the citizens' assembly. Awarding of the scholarships is supposed to be based on a needs assessment, with the poorest families first in line. Input is also requested from residents, who are asked to identify young people who should qualify based on need and potential. One student currently studying political science at the ULA had this to say:

> These scholarships are an important benefit and are an outcome of local participatory democracy because our community understands its members more than any state bureaucracy could. Through programs like this, which are local and allow residents to decide on something like who benefits from a program based on our knowledge of our own community, we can ensure that everyone has a chance to pursue their goals regardless of their socioeconomic circumstances. This is an essential element of participatory democracy.[26]

As in the other two cases, this communal council also decided on a plan to replace the roofs of homes in need of repair. The council undertook a census in order to identify families in a situation of risk; their homes were chosen as beneficiaries of the project. The process here was somewhat less participatory and dynamic than those observed in the other two cases. Whereas those cases involved a participatory process including those from families who would potentially benefit from the proposed projects, in this case the council's financial organ (consisting of five individuals elected by the assembly) selected the homes based on the results of the census. As in the other two cases, the funding process involved officials from state agencies charged with supporting participatory projects as well as citizen representatives. In these cases, the council forwarded the priorities voted on by members to *Corporación de los Andes* (Corpoandes), a body responsible for regional economic development that has a set budget for communal council funding. Each project was put into an envelope and these were evaluated as part of the "communal power cycle" process during the annual "war room" sessions. The process involves hours of debate and deliberation. These fora involve representatives from local communal councils evaluating the projects in each envelope based on a determined methodology (essentially a "greatest needs" assessment) and selecting the projects to be funded.

At the time of this research, only 10 homes had benefited from the program. This represents a relatively low number of families and individuals affected compared with the Catia and Yagua cases. At least 10 more homes were slated to be repaired, but owners had been waiting for over a year. Comments from residents about the benefits generated by their communal council were somewhat more mixed than in the other two cases. Carla, a single mother who had been selected in this process the previous year, stated:

> Well, I don't know what is taking so long. We residents decided on projects such as the replacement of roofing in 2010 and our home was later selected in a census but so far we haven't seen results. A couple of families over there on Av. 7 did have their roofs fixed in June. It is still better than before because we can use the council to exercise pressure and the council is accountable to us, we are the council. Still, we were hoping that we would see results more quickly.[27]

Characteristics of Venezuelan Communal Councils: Understanding Their Strengths and Weaknesses

What are the characteristics of these communal councils that explain the relatively successful outcomes? The cases score well on the criteria found in the participatory democracy literature, with variation in the Belén case where the outcomes were also less positive. According to residents and officials, they allow for a real devolution of decision-making to citizens at the local level, are autonomous, inclusive of groups formerly excluded from power, offer an environment conducive to real deliberation among citizens, have a high level of engagement, and provide participants with the opportunity to be involved in the implementation of their decisions. On the other hand, there are various weaknesses that support many of the criticisms of participatory democracy found in the literature. For example, while communal councils meet the criteria for inclusiveness put forward in the theoretical literature in that they provide an opportunity for marginalized groups to engage in decision making, their politicized nature means that groups not affiliated with the Bolivarian project may be (or at least feel) excluded. The relative success of these mechanisms in producing high-value outcomes establishes the importance of characteristics such as having formal decision-making powers, a process for ensuring real deliberation, inclusiveness, and high levels of participation. But while they are in some ways autonomous from local governments, they also demonstrate the dangers of politicization and ideological influence that can produce a complex relationship with the state, a relationship that may simultaneously provide marginalized citizens with agency while incorporating civil society into the state.

Devolution of Decision Making to Citizens

As discussed in chapter 3, the institutional design of Venezuelan communal councils allows participants to make their own decisions in a number of key areas related to local development. Former President Chávez set the tone for this in his 2006 speech introducing these mechanisms:

> Mayors, governors, political parties, members of the national assembly . . . and even myself . . . we should be facilitators, we should support this force from below. But the people are the boss (*el pueblo es el dueño*).[28]

Representatives of state agencies charged with overseeing popular participation unanimously contend that it is the government's intention to devolve decision-making powers to citizens and that the institutionalization of communal councils reflects this goal. Planning officials charged with decentralization and supporting participatory projects argue that Venezuela is transitioning to a participatory democracy in which citizens (rather than municipal governments) identify needs that exist within their communities and decide on solutions. They present this devolution of power as a radical change that is needed in order to achieve social development and more equitable access to public goods and services. A senior official from the Fundacomunal headquarters in Caracas explained his position in terms similar to those used by most of his colleagues:

> When it comes to decision-making at the local level, power has been transferred to citizens. They [the citizens] introduce proposals through their communal councils and from that point on, a process of participatory democracy is initiated. The role of our agency and others is to serve this process, to support popular power. The people construct their own projects, because they are the ones who understand their communities and needs.[29]

Perhaps more surprisingly, most elected officials interviewed from government and opposition parties also recognize the powers delegated to citizens and are generally accepting of the idea of full citizen control.

All Venezuelan communal councils are granted these powers, although officials admit that there is variation with respect to the extent that they are used. They suggest that in some municipalities local officials may put up more resistance, while in others participants themselves may be less willing to exercise these powers fully, preferring to rely on state agents to do the work. While local officials in Guacara and Caracas were extremely enthusiastic about the role of communal councils in the decision-making and implementation processes, those from Mérida (a non-PSUV controlled municipality) were more likely to express unease. These officials argued that they too have an important role to play and that not everything can be left up to citizen participants.

Officials representing opposition parties or non-PSUV social movement groups expressed concerns about devolution of power to communal councils due to the possibility of majority domination. A member of the Democratic Action (*Acción Democrática*, AD) party expressed a common theme that emerged in interviews with these individuals:

> We are not against the communal councils, we think that they can actually produce better, more transparent government by giving power to the average citizen. What we are worried about is how they are being used. If the majority in a given community is to be given power, then like any group in power, there must be balances to avoid using that power to trample over the rights of minorities.[30]

Citizen participants tend to agree with state officials with respect to the powers that these mechanisms should have on paper and do have in reality. They agree that these are considerable, at least within the scope of local affairs. Participants agreed that they have real powers to make decisions about matters that affect their lives and also that the initiative to form a communal council originated with community members and not with state representatives.

Closely related to the extent to which power has been devolved to communal councils is the question of their autonomy with respect to the state and/or local government, at least in terms of their defined scope of influence. Politicians and government officials (central or local) are not permitted to intervene in the decision-making process of communal councils, and participants said that the relationship between their council and state institutions is characterized by mutual respect. While technicians from various departments are deployed to support council members with the development of their projects, all of those involved insist that they do so under the direction of the communal council. As Max, an agricultural worker and council participant from Guacara relates:

> They (municipal officials) rarely try to interfere, they respect our autonomy, at least they do here. But if there is a conflict between a communal council and the mayor for example, the Ombudsman (*Defensoría del Pueblo*) can intervene and make sure that he is not imposing his will on the people[31]

To understand the extent of this devolution of powers, participants were also asked to describe the process as they have witnessed it. The vast majority were able to explain the process in detail and their responses depict a system in which citizens do play a key role. Marbella and José Luis, who have both served as *voceros*, relate how they have experienced the process:

Everything begins in the collective, made up of the executive and other voceros. They conduct needs assessments and talk to the community and then come up with proposals. They then put out a call to the community and everything is brought before the citizens' assembly so that people know what they are working on and can decide on what they want to go forward. They put out three calls, we have to get at least half of the people represented by the council plus one.[32]

Decision making and implementation happen within the council. No, local authorities don't intervene in the process, they do not come to assembly meetings, they cannot tell us what to do or change decisions once the assembly has voted, no way.[33]

Venezuelan communal councils are also distinct from participatory mechanisms in the two other countries studied here in that they play an important role in the implementation of their decisions. This is written into the institutional design which details a "communal cycle" that includes an implementation phase to ensure that councils not only make and decide on proposals but execute them. State officials place considerable emphasis on the ability of citizens to participate beyond the decision-making stage. They argue that communal councils play an important role in terms of executing and managing projects (including hiring labor, purchasing materials, monitoring progress) and point to both the institutional design of the councils and the training provided to support participants in these roles. An agent from the Corpoandes development agency explained:

The community's engagement in this process does not end when a decision has been made, it follows the policy process. So, the community must be involved in implementing the decisions they have made, evaluating and assessing the results, that is an essential part of the process, that is how people learn democracy. This also ensures accountability.[34]

In the Catia and Yagua cases, participants were actively engaged at every level of implementation, including oversight of the budget, determining costs and materials to be purchased, working with engineers to design plans and maps of work to be carried out, hiring and supervision of labor and other personnel, and inspecting work completed. Participants relied on support and advice from engineers and technicians but were responsible for oversight and day-to-day decisions (a claim corroborated by the technicians). Participants placed considerable importance on the role of communal councils in the implementation stage, generally linking these powers to the outcomes and arguing that decision-making powers would be useless if they could not subsequently operationalize their decisions. Blanca, a member of her council's executive explained:

> We have been successful because we always implement the decisions our citizens make, this is what allows us to make sure things are carried out as the people intended. Before the same thing always happened, the elected representatives and the bureaucracy implemented what they wanted. So that didn't work, but with communal councils the people participate all the way through to implementation and evaluating.[35]

Marisol, an active member of the same council agreed:

> Now the communal councils propose and manage projects themselves. We execute our decisions directly, maybe with the help of an engineer or other technician from a government agency, but we do it ourselves.[36]

Almost all of the participants who addressed the topic pointed to the efficiency of councils in implementing their own decisions and linked it to better outcomes. Henrick, a construction worker, summarize the opinions commonly expressed by his neighbors:

> Projects end up costing half as much as when the municipalities managed them. Communal councils are more efficient. Why? Because the people know what things cost, poorer people know this because we have to. We know where to go for the lowest cost materials and will go locally if possible. Also, we know how to do the work, to build things. We can do it ourselves better than those who don't know these things.[37]

In the first few years following their establishment (2006–2009), communal councils were dependent on funding from municipalities and state governments and had to develop their own means of managing whatever resources they were able to acquire. This led to complaints from citizens who were angry that the decisions they are legally entitled to make through their communal councils were being blocked by mayors and other local authorities who withheld money due to fear of losing their authority. Understanding this to be an impediment to the autonomy of the participatory system, the 2009 reform brought in important changes as described by a high-ranking official from an agency that provides support to communal councils:

> We used to get a lot of complaints from citizens who were angry that the decisions they are legally entitled to make through their communal councils were being blocked by mayors and other local authorities who didn't want to give up their powers and so withheld money for projects and things like that. So we decided that the only way to ensure that councils had the autonomy the law says they should have was to give them financial autonomy.[38]

Most participants agreed that having access to and control over their own financial resources was a key determinant of autonomy. As a member of the one of the council's financial committees put it:

> It is one thing to have these powers on paper, but they wouldn't mean much if we didn't have access to money, if we couldn't control our financial resources. It is the most important thing to make sure that we are independent.[39]

While we have seen that some opposition actors expressed concern about the influence of the central government (and in particular the PSUV itself) on communal council matters, most participants rejected the idea that communal councils are controlled or manipulated in any way by the government or party (this includes many of the participants who do not identify as *chavistas*). Respondents tended to feel that such views are propagated to delegitimize participatory mechanisms and to depict their members as unintelligent and therefore easily manipulated. These individuals tended to assert that the government does have certain lines they want communal councils to follow (deliberation and decisions are expected to focus on "common needs" and "community building" rather than on private interests) but reject that this should be read as state control of these mechanisms.

While all communal councils have the same powers on paper, these are not always exercised to the same extent. Participants in the two higher-value outcome cases agree that their councils exercise the powers they have on paper, but responses from the medium-value outcome case (Belén) reveal a more complex situation. Most agreed that they have real powers to make decisions about matters that affect their lives and that their council was sufficiently independent from any level of government, but some claimed that state institutions have made final decisions on approved projects. When asked about the relationship between local government and the council, those from the Belén case were less enthusiastic than participants in the other Venezuelan cases. Fewer were able to explain the decision-making process in detail but these respondents described their experience differently in that there has been some resistance on the part of municipal or parish-level officials. This is likely due to the fact that the municipality was controlled by an opposition party administration. The position of the municipal government is that while it supports communal council power, it also has certain responsibilities as an elected representative government and must ensure that non-PSUV supporters are not shut out of the process.[40] The council's spokespeople also described a decision-making process in which technicians from agencies such as Corpoandes played a more central role in advising and guiding participants than the process that was observed in the other Venezuelan cases.

In terms of implementation, the projects for Belén demonstrated a lower level of involvement than in the other Venezuelan cases. For the sports court and school kitchen, for example, members of the communal council held a public competition for the purposes of hiring labor and purchasing resources and equipment. For both projects, committees reviewed the proposals, selected the ones they felt offered the best value, and presented these to the citizens' assembly for a vote. Beyond this, residents of this council tended to rely more on technicians from Fundacomunal and Corpoandes for the development of plans and blueprints. Council leaders attribute this to the relatively low levels of engagement among its membership.

Respondents were also more likely to express concern over the influence of the central government and the PSUV on communal council matters. In contrast to Catia and Yagua, about one-third of Belén respondents felt this influence may be exercised indirectly, through state discourse and training programs for council participants. A doctor who had served as president of the council summed up what other non-*chavista* participants argued:

> I think there are certainly certain lines that councils have to follow to get funding, there are criteria set out by the central government. Does this mean that councils are not really autonomous and are instruments of the government? I have not seen direct intervention from a central or local government official or any attempt to impose a particular direction or decision. People wouldn't allow that . . . but does the party influence how communal council participants think about politics? Yes, I think so.[41]

Deliberation

Theorists argue that if participatory mechanisms are to provide opportunities for effective (as opposed to symbolic) participation, there must a process of meaningful deliberation and these mechanisms must provide a forum for all individuals to express their opinions freely as opposed to being merely consultative. Officials charged with oversight of popular participation in Venezuela stressed this point. A director of Fundacomunal explained:

> We designed the communal councils to be deliberative, they are designed to provide a forum for discussion among equals. We provide training to citizens so that they understand what deliberation means and how to engage in this type of discussion: it is about speaking your mind, listening to others and making decisions based on the best arguments.[42]

Participants from the three communal councils studied in this book generally agreed that deliberative institutions such as the citizens' assemblies and the various working groups they have participated in have been characterized by an open, tolerant discussion process. Participants felt that their council meetings meet the most important criteria of deliberation, that all who wish to speak may do so, that people are generally listened to when expressing their opinion, and that a variety of options are discussed and weighed. People felt this way both with respect to their own interventions in council business as well as their observations of how others were treated. It is particularly important to note that these positive experiences with respect to what they see as a rich deliberative process were expressed by both men and women and across age groups and occupation/education levels. Many who had attempted to participate in municipal meetings prior to the creation of communal councils compared the latter experience very favorably with the former. When asked directly about their experience, most expressed something similar to what Iris, a council participant and domestic worker, explained:

> In the citizen assemblies, we are all the same, there are no hier-archies, and everyone knows this. So yes, in these places we can have our say, we can discuss with our own neighbours. Before, when we only had municipalities, nobody listened to us when we tried to express an opinion, those were not deliberative.[43]

Council *voceros* also recognized their role in ensuring a deliberative environment. According to Helen, who served as the president of her council:

> Within the communal council, the ultimate authority is the citizen assembly and this is by nature a deliberative body, its purpose is to allow for deliberation among equal citizens. There are elected spokespeople, but they are only there to propose things. We have to follow the rules and norms, if we don't, if we try to impose our own opinion, the people won't allow that, they know they have the right to be heard and listened to.[44]

Some respondents also provided more detail about the nature of deliberation itself, and while they do not engage directly with Habermasian concepts, most responses suggest that people take seriously the idea of the "force of the better argument."

> We discuss problems of the community, common problems. There has to be deliberation because we must determine what the most important common problems are in order to move forward, this requires people to propose arguments based on what is best for everyone. This is much more deliberative that representative institutions where everyone just argues for their

own interests or the interests of the group they represent, that is easy enough to do. But making an argument in favour of what is best for everyone, that is much harder, that requires real deliberation.[45]

Many referred to the self-regulating nature of the councils, arguing that members themselves insist on ensuring the deliberative nature:

> We see deliberation as figuring out what is best for everyone, deliberating and listening to everyone's ideas about how to meet the needs of the most people. Some people do sometimes start talking about personal problems they want the council to solve, that is normal. But they can't go far if they are just focused on private interests, the group dynamic won't allow that.[46]

Participants were also asked specifically about whether or not leaders emerge (informally if not formally) within the councils and to what extent these individuals may dominate the debate and therefore pose a threat to the deliberative nature of the process. While many admitted that informal leaders emerge and that some individuals occasionally attempt to impose their will, these participants argued that the participatory nature of the mechanisms, the lack of formal hierarchies, and the group dynamic are all factors that prevent one or more individuals from dominating the process. As one participant put it:

> There are people who try to dominate sometimes, that is how people are. But they can't dominate the entire process because they don't make decisions, they can only put their ideas forward and there are procedures in place to make sure everyone gets a chance to talk. In any case, the actual decisions are made in the citizens' assembly so even if someone is louder than everyone else, it doesn't mean they will get their way.[47]

Some individuals did express concern that personal and group rivalries sometimes have a negative impact on deliberation within the council, and a few felt (contrary to the majority opinion) that some individuals tend to dominate. The latter perspective was more common among participants in Belén and can perhaps be explained in part by lower participation levels there. With respect to rivalries, former council president Marbella illustrates the type of problem mentioned by some of those who identified this as a problem.

> Well, people do have personal goals and some try to use these places to advance those. This creates rivalries where someone says 'I want this' and someone else wants something else. In Venezuela there are many divisions and when people start to act this way it can harm the deliberative process because then they don't base their arguments on needs, people start to push their own desires over those of others, forgetting that the common good should prevail. When this happens it can really damage what the deliberative process is supposed to be.[48]

Others expanded on a perception that despite the formal rules and procedures, some people do manage to dominate the discussion and influence decision making more than others.

> It shouldn't be, but it happens. There is a group of people who participate more, who are known in the community, who are seen as leaders and who want to dominate the process. They try to influence the decision making process and sometimes this happens because they have influence over people, people will listen to them and repeat what they say. But often this is because they participate more and know more about what is going on, so it sounds like they know what they are talking about.[49]

Still, even these individuals tended to point out that regardless of these problems, the communal councils provide a forum far more conducive to public deliberation than liberal-representative ones, which the generally associate with the system of "the past." While few of the regular participants were of the opinion that councils are not at all deliberative, a number of non-participants interviewed (generally associated with opposition parties) did make this argument. Those who expressed this opinion also admitted, however, that they neither participate nor have they ever participated in a communal council. Rather, they claim that their experience as non-chavista citizens leads them to believe that they would not be listened to if they were to participate. As we have seen, the concerns were most commonly expressed in the case with lower participation rates. Given that participants in Yagua and especially Catia cases were likely to attribute the deliberative nature of their own councils to the group dynamic and high participation rate, it is likely that level of participation does indeed play a role in determining how deliberative these mechanisms are; the fewer people who engage regularly, the easier it is for those who do participate to dominate the process.

Inclusiveness

State discourse in Venezuela frames inclusiveness as incorporating the participation of those who previously had no access points (the poor, the less well-educated, women, Afro-Venezuelans). The idea was expressed by Chávez himself; in his earliest speech describing the purpose of these mechanisms, he declared that "communal councils should develop from below, from popular assemblies in the barrios" and that they were part of a reorganization of power intended to include the majority in decision making as opposed to small elite groups of the past.[50] This is the main argument that most politicians and public servants interviewed put forward when asked about communal councils. Government officials stressed the contrast between the current system and what they perceive to be an exclusive and exclusionary system of the past, arguing that under representative institutions only a few people made decisions (the socioeconomic elite) and that while everyone had the right to vote, this type of limited participation does not equate with inclusiveness if those elected only represent the interests of a few. They claim that the new system of participation allows average citizens a say in decisions that affect their lives. An adviser to the minister responsible for communal councils explained:

> This is the most important goal of the Bolivarian Revolution: allowing people who have always been excluded from power to have a say. The communal councils were designed to be in every neighbourhood, to give everyone an equal chance to participate regardless of status, education, gender, skin colour. This is why there are no hierarchal relationships built in to the structure. And we know that even the poorest citizens are represented, we know that women participate in great numbers.[51]

The data collected for these cases demonstrate that the vast majority of participants are from "traditionally excluded" groups. Over half of respondents were women. With respect to socioeconomic status, the largest number of respondents (26%) can be identified as precarious/unskilled workers (generally in the informal sector). This category included many informal sector construction workers and domestic workers. Other common categories include homemakers (24%), retail workers, educators, and tradespeople. In terms of income, a majority of informants (72%) earned at or below the monthly minimum wage of 2,973 Bs.F.[52] In terms of demographic composition, the Belén communal council is more middle-income in nature, with a minority (41%) of participants earning less than the monthly minimum wage of 2,973 Bs.F (compared with 72% in Catia and Yagua).

The vast majority of Catia and Yagua participants believed that the councils are inclusive mechanisms in that they have been successful in engaging economically marginalized groups and those with little formal education, and they leverage the experience and abilities of all citizens. The opinions expressed revolved around the belief that in the past there was no importance placed on the opinion of the average person, the poor, and working people in that all decisions were made behind closed doors and at a higher level. Participants claimed that it was never clear what these individuals discussed or how they made decisions, but those directly affected were rarely included. This, they claim, had a predictable impact on access to public goods and services, with those belonging to the same social groups as the decision makers receiving the benefits. Raquel, an Afro-Venezuelan teacher and council *vocera* who had grown up in a makeshift dwelling, expressed an opinion similar to that of her neighbors:

> Before there was no importance placed on the opinion of someone like me. Everything, all decisions happened at a higher level and who knows how they made decisions or what they discussed but they never included the people who are actually affected, we are just poor and stupid according to them. Not anymore. If some[one] has the time and the will, they can participate and be heard regardless of background.[53]

Class was often brought up as a factor in the interviews; many participants expressed sentiments similar to Fer, a shoe salesman who grew up on the streets of a popular *barrio* in Caracas and now serves as a *vocero*:

The essential component of the Bolivarian Revolution and participatory democracy is inclusion, of the masses, the working people, the majority. There has been empowerment through these institutions and others such as the missions, we are not passive anymore. We are conscious of our capacity to change our reality. We can feel it in our communal councils, in our popular organizations. There is class consciousness in the country and communal councils are at the centre of this.[54]

Others, particularly in the semi-rural Guacara case, specifically mentioned participation being opened to people with less formal education. Juan Carlos, a formerly landless agricultural worker, made this common observation:

There are people in our community, especially older people, who don't know how to read well, but they love their country, they are committed to their community so why shouldn't they have as much of a voice as the educated? Now they can through communal councils which are open to everyone.[55]

And council participant Geraldina stated:

A lot of people around here don't have a high level of education . . . and aren't very qualified (*preparado*) but they do have dreams and goals and deserve to have a say. Under the old system only the qualified and professionals had the right to make decisions, now everyone can have a say.[56]

Related to this, a number of participants pointed to the training available to communal council participants as well as the hands-on experience as an essential element of Venezuela's participatory democracy model. They argue that education and training are important in terms of ensuring inclusiveness in that it helps to even the playing field. Previously, it was easier for middle-class, educated people to participate because they had the skills, political knowledge, and ability to articulate themselves clearly. The communal system provides everyone relevant training and experience, including how to make a budget, how to write a project proposal, and how to participate in meetings. As Fer insists, "this allows everyone to participate, not just those with qualifications (*gente preparada*) and has resulted in the more equitable local policy outcomes."[57]

A significant majority of women believed that they play a leading role in communal councils. Certain common themes emerged from the women interviewed. Many claimed that representative institutions (national assemblies, municipal councils) are and have always been dominated by men; participatory mechanisms allow women the opportunity to make their voices heard. Also, many female respondents claimed that they feel more comfortable speaking and participating in a group that includes as many or more women than men. They feel they are more likely to be taken seriously, less likely to have their opinions dismissed, and that participatory mechanisms provide such a forum due to high participation rates among women. As Laura, a cook who sells food at a street stall in her *barrio*, explains: "There are more women than men in this process. The face of the revolution is the face of a woman; women have played a leading role (*rol protagónico*) in communal councils, but also beyond."[58] Many of the women use the past as a reference point, arguing that they have a far greater role to play in decision making through these local mechanisms than they did in a recent past dominated by exclusionary institutions. As Geraldina, a domestic worker who has served in various capacities on her communal councils, insists:

> The municipality used to have meetings open to the public, for consultation. The representatives there from the city were mostly men, they treated women like children, especially those of us who are not very educated (*preparadas*). I only went once and saw how they treated women who tried to express an opinion so I didn't speak and never went again. In the communal council citizens' assembly it is different, there are as many women as men, I feel comfortable, it is a place where discussion is encouraged and we feel good about it.[59]

While only a handful of respondents self-identified as Afro-Venezuelan, these individuals also claimed that communal councils have provided them with a forum where they can discuss issues with their fellow citizens in a context devoid of the hierarchies and barriers of the traditional political institutions. As Raquel explains:

> Another thing that is not talked about is that there is a lot of racism in Venezuela. Here in Carabobo there has always been a large Afro population but do you think we used to see our-

selves represented in the old institutions? Do you think they ever included us? No. I can say that I do feel that we have more of a voice now, I have participated in the communal council since it began and I have the same voice as everyone else. I don't feel like my neighbours don't pay attention to us for that reason, not the way the old institutions used to ignore us.[60]

Not all Venezuelans feel they have a place in their neighborhood's communal council, however. While participants are clearly drawn from the popular sectors (which is the stated intention of the government's participatory democracy agenda), they also tend to be individuals who are inclined to support the government. We have already seen that data on participants studied in this project confirm this trend; the majority of participants identify as dedicated *chavistas* and many have participated in other initiatives launched by Chávez's government such as the various missions that provide social services and educational opportunities. This has led opposition parties and media sources to label the institutions as being overly partisan. Some individuals interviewed, who identified as opposition supporters, expressed this concern about exclusion based on political allegiance. While most acknowledged that communal councils have expanded participatory opportunities to the poor and women, several insisted that non-*chavistas* are effectively excluded from the deliberative process. Angel, an occasional member of the Belén communal council said:

> I guess they are more inclusive in some ways. Yes, certain people who were left out before now have a voice. But to be truly inclusive, they should include everyone, of any political leanings and should even include the middle classes because they are still part of our society.[61]

Most participants stressed that non-*chavistas* have participated in assembly meetings, that they have not been deliberately excluded, and that the benefits are extended to everyone in the community. Leandro, a member of his council's executive argued:

> Is there exclusion or discrimination? No, I have not seen it. Look, when neighbourhoods are improved, opposition supporters still benefit from the projects. Improvements to infrastructure, to drinking water, these things are good for

everyone. We don't exclude people from that, projects are by area, they are general. If people choose to exclude themselves from the decision and planning process, that is their choice.[62]

Many respondents also complained that opponents of participatory mechanisms (whom they characterize as the displaced elites) wish to reverse the process because they intend to (re)exclude the poor from decision making. As one Caracas participant put it:

The opposition says that communal councils are corrupt because they associate them with the poor and they think the poor are corrupt and ignorant (*brutos*). Well let me say that the middle classes and the rich are also corrupt, before they used to keep all of the state oil revenue to themselves and exclude the rest of us. They want to go back to that way of doing things. But that will not happen now that we have a role in deciding how money gets spent, we won't be excluded again.[63]

Levels of Participation

Overall, lack of participation is seen as less of a problem in Venezuela than in Chile and Ecuador (where it tends to be lower), yet it is still identified as one of the most significant characteristics in the success of a communal council by both observers and participants themselves. Certainly, the outcomes (both hard and soft) align with participation levels: the most successful cases demonstrate the highest levels and most sustained engagement, while the case which has achieved the least (Belén) has fared comparatively poorly on these factors.

Government officials and citizen participants stress that the level of participation and engagement is an important factor to consider in understanding the outcomes. If the rate of participation is low or wanes over time, the councils can essentially be taken over by a handful of *voceros*, but high and sustained levels of community involvement encourage the development of the other factors discussed above. They argue that the number of active participants can vary from over 200 to as few as 10 and this is a significant factor in terms of the council's ability to provide a deliberative forum for discussion, to be inclusive as well as to use its capacity to implement and evaluate projects. A project manager affiliated with Fundacomunal sums up how most officials view this factor:

The most important thing is participation and the level of commitment. In some councils, a few people do all the work. If Juan doesn't do it, nothing gets done. In successful councils, if Juan doesn't do it, Maria and Pedro will. And in any case, participation is essential to achieving any kind of participatory democracy; if people don't get involved, it will just become another representative institution.[64]

The three cases demonstrate an alignment between participation levels and the extent and scope of outcomes. The Catia case presents a very high level of participation and commitment. A significant percentage of the represented citizens were currently engaged in the council and this involvement has been sustained over time according to spokespeople and attendance records for the citizens' assembly. Of the approximately 350 families represented, over 90 individuals have participated in various committees and working groups and an average of 140 attend the citizens' assembly. These numbers have remained relatively stable over the past four years. We have also seen that this case saw the most significant results and that decisions were most likely to be implemented and projects carried through and sustained.

Yagua also demonstrates a high level of participation. An average of 80 to 90 people attend the citizens' assembly on a regular basis, although this attendance has fluctuated over the past three years. Members are more likely to attend and participate during the decision-making stage, but commitment tends to diminish once people have gotten what they want. In the Belén case, participation has also varied over time, yet the trend has been for active involvement to decline over time. Fewer individuals participate regularly in committees (only 12 individuals from the over 200 families represented have been involved at this level) and attendance at assemblies has also steadily diminished. Only around 20 have attended the past few meetings. *Voceros* attribute this to lack of time and interest on the part of their neighbors. This may be problematic from the perspective of the *voceros* (who must assume the burden) but also confirms some of the concerns raised by skeptics about the feasibility of expecting people to participate in a sustained manner.

State-Society Relationships

The "radical" participatory mechanisms known as communal councils possess a number of characteristics that have the potential to strengthen civil society and to encourage citizenship as agency. They provide opportunities for genuine deliberation and inclusion of traditionally marginalized groups, yet the nature of the relationship between these mechanisms and the state introduces dangers of cooptation and controlled inclusion. While citizen participants believe that they are autonomous in their internal decision-making process, there are lingering questions about the level of indirect influence that the state is able to have on the participatory process. The entire system of communal councils is under the oversight of a central government ministry, the *Ministerio del Poder Popular para las Comunas y los Movimientos Sociales* (MPComunas). To officially establish a council, founding members must apply for and receive recognition from MPComunas, although legally this permission is only a formality if they have proceeded according to the law.

Communal councils also tend to be politicized in that most individuals who choose to participate are supporters of the "Bolivarian Revolution" and the ruling PSUV. These factors mean that it is possible for the central level to have at least an indirect influence on communal councils. Furthermore, the focus of councils is strictly at the local level, with participants either working with municipal officials or using the powers allotted to them to bypass local elected officials and civil servants deemed to be ineffectual. Individuals and civil society therefore tend to be highly mobilized at the local level (often against local governments, particularly when these are controlled by opposition parties) but not against the central level. All of this creates an uneven relationship with a mobilized, engaged civil society at the local level that has little influence at the central level in terms of policy.

The composition of the three cases does reflect the partisan nature of the participatory institutions in that most respondents are government supporters. While participants are clearly drawn from the popular sectors (which is the stated intention of the governments' participatory democracy agenda), they also tend to be individuals who are inclined to support the government.[65] Most individuals interviewed who identified as opposition supporters expressed this concern about exclusion based on political allegiance. Exclusion (whether intentional or not) from mechanisms intended to foster interaction between civil society and the state may force organizations to decide between cooptation and being excluded from the policymaking process. Politicization appears to be a reality that carries the risk of endangering many of the qualities that make these participatory mechanisms successful (such as inclusiveness). A leader of an opposition-oriented social movement argued that:

The CCs are the continuation of a model that was already developing within civil society, the neighbourhood associations but they have a more political character which allows them to be manipulated. On paper and in some ways, they have autonomy but at the same time this politicization undermines their autonomy.[66]

Participants who support the government's participatory democracy agenda are more likely than non-supporters to experience positive spill-over effects. These citizens highly value the experience of participation in and of itself. They claim that they feel more positive about democracy in Venezuela and their ability to have a say than in the past; most feel they have considerable freedom of choice and control over their lives and generally agree that they and their neighbors are able to be heard and to influence political decisions.

Citizen participation, the existence of participatory mechanisms, and the related ability to participate in decisions affecting their lives was most often cited as the reason for this enhanced sense of empowerment. Of those who expressed a positive assessment of the state of democracy in Venezuela, a majority provided some variation on this theme. Most simply mentioned "citizen participation" or "popular participation" (*participación ciudadana, participación popular*); others were more specific (i.e., "we can participate in the decision-making process"). This is perhaps not surprising considering the involvement of the surveyed individuals in participatory institutions, but it does attest to the importance that they place on citizen participation in decision making. Residents also identified expanded inclusion as significant. This centers around the belief that a wider segment of the population is able to exert influence on government than in the past. A statement provided by a teacher in Guacara is typical of the sentiments expressed:

> It used to be that communities had to wait for everything to be solved by elected authorities at the national level or in the mayor's office. Maybe we would benefit from their decisions, but more often we wouldn't. Not anymore. Now, if citizens have the time and good will, we can make our own decisions, we can go and participate and have a voice.[67]

Women participants are even more likely to develop positive feelings about democracy and a greater sense of political efficacy than men. Nearly half of the female respondents mentioned something to do with the role of women. Miriana, a Caracas communal council participant, expressed a sentiment similar to that of many of her peers:

> We (women) are busy, we work, we have families. Councils are in our neighbourhoods, they are close to us, it is easy to participate for anyone who wants to. I think this is why so many women participate . . . and also because we want to have a voice, we want to be heard. Where else is this going to happen? Certainly not in the municipal councils. So when women participate, we all feel better prepared to participate and we know we will be listened to in our councils.[68]

Anita, a kitchen worker, provided some insight on the added value of participating in communal councils that many of those with lower levels of formal education expressed:

> Being part of the (communal) council, we learn so much about government works, about what agency does what, about who to contact to get this or that done. This allows us to be more useful participants not only in the council but in other organizations, we know how to get things done and who in the government can help us get things done.[69]

While most citizen participants experienced positive spillover effects, those who do not identify strongly with the ruling PSUV are less inclined to hold the favorable views expressed in the broader sample. In a statement typical of the opinions expressed by this group, one former communal council participant in Belén said:

> The process of decision-making inside of the communal councils has to follow the presidential line; there is no room for those who would oppose the plans or ideology of the national government.[70]

The terms used by citizen participants align with those produced by state institutions, suggesting that participatory mechanisms act to socialize people into participating in "legitimate" and acceptable ways.

Individuals have a particular understanding of what democracy is and is not. Throughout the interviews, popular participation is contrasted with representative democracy in a manner that frames the former as noble and productive and the latter as corrupt and ineffective. Democracy itself is conceived of in terms of its variants. References to democracy are preceded or followed by qualifiers such as "participatory," "real," "social," and "popular," on the one hand, or "representative," "past," "false." and "elite," on the other. The former terms are associated with the ability of citizens to exercise agency while the latter are linked discursively to passive citizenship and exclusion. The use of "popular" as a positive descriptor was common. Uses include popular will (often contrasted with "selfish" private interests), popular sovereignty (often contrasted with elite dominance), and popular power (often contrasted with rule by the few). These terms were generally applied in an adversarial context in which "el pueblo" is required to defend itself against right-wing and/or elite forces determined to strip the average citizen of her power, as in the assertion that "the right constantly tries to block popular power," commonly expressed.

Examining how participants understand the role of citizens in the context of participatory democracy also reveals certain patterns. While participants rarely engaged directly with how they understand these concepts, the context in which they discuss them does provide some clues. "The citizen" was most frequently framed in collective terms and linked discursively to participation, dignity and equality. Common examples include assertions that the citizen "unites around objectives aimed at the common good," "feels a commitment to achieving community goals," "participates in decisions that affect their lives and their communities," and "should be equal to everyone else." When using the term "el pueblo," respondents tended to reproduce the discursive patterns of state actors and institutions that identify "good" and "bad" categories. They associate "el pueblo" with "real people," "working people," and "simple people," but their responses were almost always presented in contrast to The Other. The Other is often defined as the "elite" but just as frequently as "the opposition," and participants rarely distinguished between leaders and followers of "the opposition." Such people (not included in "el pueblo") are generally discussed in antagonistic terms.

Representatives and representative democracy are viewed as illegitimate and self-serving. In fact, most participants who did mention local officials expressed hostility toward them and their representative institutions, insisting that they would not participate in the council if they felt these individuals were involved. Francisco expressed the frustrations of many of his neighbors:

> Mayors and governors and their bureaucracies . . . they are the cancer of the system, of the entire revolutionary process, they still have too much power. But the communal councils have more and more autonomy, more powers every year, their power continues to grow.[71]

This Rousseauian conception of democracy closely mirrors the discursive patterns found both in legislation and participatory training materials in Venezuela, which emphasize citizen involvement in decision making and socioeconomic equality over procedural quality.[72]

Another important and related consideration is the scope of participation that is deemed relevant and "available" for public participation. The discourse transmitted through participatory mechanisms establishes strict parameters around citizenship with respect to both acceptable forms of participation and the mechanisms through which engagement should ideally be exercised. The sphere in which councils can participate is focused on local needs such as improved infrastructure and social development. While these mechanisms do have the power to engage in decisions beyond local infrastructure and public works projects, the cases studied here have not exercised such prerogatives and, in any case, their influence can rarely extend beyond the community. Thus far, questions of national importance remain outside of the purview of participatory mechanisms. A number of respondents, both supporters and non-supporters, also expressed a broader view about the focus of communal councils on overly practical and technical affairs to the detriment of political matters. These individuals tended to point out that the stated intention of these mechanisms is to provide citizens with both a greater role in everyday decisions that affect their lives and to expand political participation (broadly defined) to "the people," yet there is consensus that while the former has been achieved, the latter goal lags behind. Many individuals, for example, lamented the inability of citizens to engage in the political arena around matters such as fiscal policy or "moral" issues. A militant from Caracas expressed these sentiments this way:

> Power has certainly been transferred to us when it comes to these things (local projects and services) and that is good

because these things affect our daily lives. But participatory democracy—and communal councils are supposed to be the mechanisms through we exercise this—is about more than that. We want to use them to create a new, more equal and democratic society and this means expanding what they do and the issues they deal with to the entire political spectrum.

Many of these individuals were concerned about extending participatory democracy to higher-level policy areas, something which the regional bodies do not adequately address. A teacher from Mérida reflects this concern:

Yes, it is important that we are able to make decisions about our own communities, but what is lacking at this point is public participation in higher-level issues. I'll give you an example: many women want to debate the question of abortion, which is still illegal in Venezuela. Well, the communal councils do not allow us to engage in such a debate. They aren't designed for that and they are focused on local issues. The regional and national citizens' assemblies tend to talk about economic issues, larger-scale socioproductive projects, things like that. So where can we citizens participate in debate over the question of abortion? There are no mechanisms for that, these things are still in the hands of legislators, of representatives. For a truly participatory democracy, devolution needs to include everything.[73]

There is therefore the danger that these institutions will become mere instruments for transferring funds to community and civil society groups, a development that downplays the important function of deepening democracy and ultimately weakens the capacity of civil society to engage in high-level issues. Taken together, the hostility toward representatives and liberal institutions, support for the central government and its participatory democracy discourse, and the local focus of communal councils mean that civil society is well organized at the local level but weak when it comes to engaging with the central level. The argument that participants are manipulated should not be overstated as it devalues these individuals' capacity to think critically and deprives them of agency. Respondents were very familiar with the powers of communal councils that allow for the devolution of decision making, and they are extremely vigilant about the possibility of any outside authority intervening in the process. Nevertheless, the fact that most participants do support the ruling party and subscribe to the state's ideology of 21st Century Socialism does mean that the framework through which they view politics is highly influenced by the central government. This may limit and shape the range of options they consider, offering the government an indirect influence in the affairs of communal councils even when state agents do not directly intervene. This may also have an impact on the quality of deliberation, which on the surface appears to be open and productive but may be constrained by the shared ideological convictions of the majority of participants.

Conclusions

In Venezuela, what is on paper is at least to some extent translated into practice when it comes to decision making about local issues that affect the lives of citizens (see summary in table 4.3). People are able to use the powers attributed to communal councils to get what they want, and active involvement has a positive impact on citizens' perceptions of democracy and sense of empowerment.

Despite problems, these councils comes closest to demonstrating the fulfillment of characteristics that theorists have argued are important in the success of participatory mechanisms: devolution of power, deliberation, inclusiveness, and high levels of participation. Participants generally link these qualities to both tangible outcomes and to their positive perceptions of democracy. These characteristics are somewhat weaker in the case that demonstrates less positive outcomes (Belén). Some of the concerns expressed by skeptics of popular participation are more prominent in this case: lower levels of participation and social organization, for example, which in turn have an effect on the capacity of the council to be fully deliberative and inclusive. These characteristics and how they contribute to the outcomes discussed earlier in this chapter will be compared to the characteristics of participatory mechanisms in Chile and Ecuador in the following two chapters. We will see, both within and across countries, that the presence or absence of these characteristics is key in determining successful outcomes, but relationships between participatory mechanisms and local government are also an important variable.

There are, however, a number of important problems that must be acknowledged. While the extent to which state penetration and control of

Table 4.3. Projects, Processes, and Outcomes, Venezuela

	Alternatives Selected	Process	Outcomes
Sucre	• Deteriorating infrastructure (sewage and drainage, water supply) • Structural deterioration of homes and residential buildings • Security concerns	Participants identify alternatives and select priorities Participants make final decisions Participants play a major role in obtaining funding	• Reconstruction of drainage and sewage systems benefiting over 200 families • Updating of water system benefiting 238 families • Housing improvements (roofing) for 30 buildings (450 families) • Establishment of a liaison program with local police detachment
Guaraca	• Poor housing conditions, particularly for recent arrivals living on "invaded" lots • Lack of utilities (electricity and sewage) • Unpaved streets • Deeds needed for families living on plots of land	Implementation carried out by participants Participants assert decision-making role in relationship with local authorities	• 50 homes built, another 30 in the planning stages, 250 people benefited • Electrification provided to 100 homes • 80 septic tanks purchased and installed • Paving of 50 streets • Obtained deeds for plots of land for 70 families

continued on next page

Table 4.3. *Continued.*

	Alternatives Selected	Process	Outcomes
Mérida	• Housing improvements (roofing) • Sports court • Eating facilities for the school • Grants to study for locals	Participants identify alternatives and select priorities Participants make final decisions Participants play a role in obtaining funding Implementation carried out by both participants and state agencies Participants assert decision-making role in relationship with local authorities but allow officials some involvement	• Housing improvements approved, not yet completed • Sports court completed • Dining room and kitchen (with equipment) built for school, over 200 children benefited • Grants for 20 students

communal councils perceived by critics may be exaggerated, politicization appears to be a reality that carries the risk of endangering many of the qualities that make these participatory mechanisms successful (autonomy, deliberation, and inclusiveness). Furthermore, while communal councils are certainly inclusive on many levels and represent an improvement over the closed institutions of the past, the possibility that nongovernment supporters are excluded (whether by their own choice or not) limits these mechanisms' capacity to include all voices in Venezuelan society. While a large segment of society that has traditionally been excluded from decision making now has opportunities to participate at the local level, a different group of citizens may in fact be excluded. Finally, while they do produce participatory democracy at the local level, they may also establish parameters around participation with respect to both acceptable forms of participation and the mechanisms through which this should be exercised.

Participants themselves are aware of most of these deficiencies but do not believe that they negate the benefits. The vast majority view participatory democracy as an evolving process and hope that some of the weaknesses will be addressed over time by the citizens themselves in collaboration with supportive state actors. Many pointed out that it is impossible to transition from a system of representative to participatory democracy in less than a decade and that a full transition will require far more time and will likely involve many mistakes. As one *vocero* stated,

> we are building a participatory democracy but we need more than 4 or 6 years. Even so, it is remarkable what we have accomplished in so little time . . . it is a beautiful thing when we can discuss with our neighbours what is best for the community, not just think about pushing our own interests.[74]

5

Ecuador

Radical Discourse, Dashed Expectations

Ecuador's so-called Citizen's Revolution ushered in by President Rafael Correa promises to put the interests of "people over capital" through various political and socioeconomic reforms. As in Venezuela, expanding opportunities for citizens to participate in politics is at the heart of this movement. While central state agencies charged with implementing participatory initiatives have promoted citizen participation, local authorities have resisted what they see as incursions into their areas of responsibility by citizens who do not have the knowledge or expertise to understand the complexities of local governance. In contrast to Venezuela, local power and municipalities are strong in Ecuador, one of the first counties in the region to decentralize. There is also a limited history of institutionalized popular participation in the country. These factors, combined with the relatively restricted powers given to participatory mechanisms, create inevitable conflict between citizens (sometimes backed up by central government agencies) who are familiar with the "on paper" rights granted to them by the constitution, and local officials who continue to see themselves as responsible for decision making.

Overall, the characteristics of Venezuelan communal councils that made them successful are not observable to the same extent in Ecuador's local citizens' assemblies. While they are generally deemed to be more inclusive than traditional representative institutions when it comes to participation of the poor, indigenous residents claim that they reproduce the same form of discrimination they have experienced elsewhere. Compared to Venezuelan communal councils, the assemblies lack autonomy and implementation powers vis-à-vis local governments and suffer from poor relationships with local authorities. They also have lower levels of participation and (perhaps as a result) the quality of internal deliberation suffers.

There is a notable disconnect between state discourse and legislation, on the one hand, and how the institutions function in reality, on the other. This produces tension between participants and local authorities as citizens' expectations of what their participatory mechanisms should do are not realized in their day-to-day operation. This tension damages the relationship between participants and local authorities, thus further reducing the role of the former in decision making and implementation.

The Cases

The first local assembly is located in the Llano Chico sector of Calderón, a municipality on the outskirts of Quito. It is primarily residential and contains both suburban and rural zones, although in recent years it has seen economic development in the form of light industry. The area is characterized by mixed socioeconomic indicators. According to the 2010 census, 27% of the population had unsatisfied basic necessities, just slightly above the average for Greater Quito.[1] The indigenous population is 7%, which is higher than the Quito average of 4%. The local assembly represents about 130 families, many of which are headed by women who have recently migrated from rural areas in search of work. The assembly is also characterized by the most diverse socioeconomic structure of any of the cases studied in this book. The neighborhood includes a mix of both more established suburban/semi-rural neighborhoods and newly built shantytowns. Many homes in the neighborhood represented by the local assembly lack basic services and infrastructure such as paved roads, while other residents live in established neighborhoods. Employment categories vary; many residents are informal laborers and domestic workers, while those who live in the more established areas include some business owners.

The second case is situated in the rural village of San Gabriel in the agricultural highlands of Carchi province near the Colombian border. The local assembly represents the canton's population of about 28,000 people and has about 100 active members, although participation varies. Participants live in small towns or in outlying rural zones. Some homes in the neighborhood represented by the local assembly lack basic services and infrastructure such as paved roads. The majority of participants work in agriculture. The third local assembly is located in Tarqui, one of the urban parishes of Manta, a mid-sized city located on the coast. Manta is one of Ecuador's most important ports and a center of its fishing industry. The Tarqui parish is urban but working class and 53% of the population is considered poor.[2] The local assembly represents the population of the parish (60,000) but has about 200 registered members. Typical of the coastal zone, people represented by this assembly are *mestizo* and there are no indigenous residents. Homes in the neighborhood are in varying states of repair but have access to basic utilities and infrastructure. The most common occupations include laborers, manufacturing and construction workers and retail service personnel. Many work in the fishing industry either as fishermen or packers.

Outcomes

Ecuador's system of citizen participation is inspired by the Venezuelan prototype, but the three local mechanisms studied here have been less successful with respect to achieving significant outcomes, and we see little evidence of the type of citizen decision making and implementation observed in Venezuela. While the central government has made historic investments in social development, this has remained a top-down form of redistribution carried out by state agencies, and there is little evidence that citizens are able to play a significant role through local participatory mechanisms. In the three cases discussed in this chapter, there is weak alignment between outcomes and participants' preferred alternatives, scope is limited, and the material conditions of residents have not improved significantly as a result of the assemblies (see table 5.1). The process that residents describe is very different from that observed in Venezuela and restricts citizens to a secondary role in decision making and implementation. Citizens are less likely to describe themselves as having real powers to make decisions about local matters and more likely to observe that government institutions make the final decisions. Not surprisingly, spillover effects are also less pronounced. While most are satisfied with the direction the country has taken, they are not pleased with how participation is working (or not working) at the local level.

Table 5.1. Outcome Evaluation Criteria, Ecuador

Case	Tangible Outcomes	Alignment with Alternatives	Scope	Improvement to Quality of Life	Participants' Role in Participatory Relationship	Participants' Role Aligns with Institutional Design
Tarqui	Medium-Low value	*Weak-Moderate*	*Moderate*	*Moderate*	Subordinate, mostly conflictual	No
San Gabriel	Low value	*Weak*	*Small*	*Minimal*	Subordinate, conflictual	No
Llano Chico	Low value	*None*	*Small*	*Minimal*	Subordinate, conflictual (and conflictual between participants)	No

Tarqui

The Tarqui citizens' assembly demonstrated modest outcomes. Citizens in this working-class urban parish identified a number of alternatives through their participatory process, many related to deteriorating public infrastructure. These include construction or re-construction of streets and sidewalks, installing public lighting, repairing storm drains, and beautification projects such as creating parks. The most pressing priorities defined by citizen participants, however, involved specific problems that affect residents' quality of life. The two river channels that cross the parish and empty into the city's port suffer from high levels of pollution. This, combined with a sewage system that has deteriorated in some sections of the parish, is seen as a major health concern. The drinking water system is considered "uneven," with some families requiring "alternative means" of securing drinking water. Residents also believe that the main public primary school in the parish is in poor physical condition and that this presents health and safety issues for the children who attend.[3]

At the time of research, modest infrastructure outcomes could be traced to the work of the local citizens' assembly. The public works projects cost just over 1,400,000 USD.[4] These included street paving, building and repairing sidewalks, creating parks, and finishing the construction of a community center. The water distribution system is in the process of being updated in parts of the parish. Municipal documents demonstrate that while Tarqui is not the most populous sector of the city, more money was spent on average than in Manta's other urban parishes.[5] However, residents had not made significant progress on the alternatives they had voted to prioritize in their local assembly. At the time of research, no attempts to address the pollution issue had been made, the sewage and water systems continued to deteriorate, and the schools had not been renovated.

A majority of participants agreed that the modest results they managed to achieve could be attributed to the local assembly, with respondents insisting that things were even worse before the existence of participatory mechanisms. Municipal officials believe that a combined effort (citizens and municipal officials) was most effective. The latter tended to frame this as a positive example of popular participation. As one municipal councillor stated:

> Our relationship with the local assemblies has varied over time but when we are able to work with them, that is when we are able to achieve things. You see the money that has been invested and the list of projects . . . that is a result of the municipality working with citizen participation mechanisms.[6]

The CPCCS participation specialist for Manabí province, who claimed that the participatory process is new and evolving but that the moderate gains observed here are a result of a devoted citizens' assembly, corroborated participants' beliefs. Citizens emphasized that while some outcomes were encouraging, they fell well below the community's expectations. They attribute this to the unequal relationship between the assembly and the municipality, which they feel makes participation less significant than it could be.

The participatory process demonstrates a relatively limited role for the local citizens' assembly when compared with Venezuelan communal councils. At the earliest stage of project initiation, assemblies were convened by communicating with residents through local media and inviting everyone living in the area to attend. Beyond this phase, the process diverges from those observed in Venezuela. While the assembly itself engaged in a deliberative process and produced decisions that most participants agreed with, it was only able to move its decisions forward to obtain funding on the projects mentioned above; it failed in achieving the assembly's more highly prioritized goals. Unlike in the Venezuelan cases, the assembly does not have implementation and oversight powers and must depend on the will of local authorities. The relationship between the assembly and municipal authorities wavers between mistrust and reluctant cooperation. Manta's decision makers did provide funding for a number of the alternatives residents had identified, but opted to invest in a series of smaller-scale capital projects, a position which residents attribute to the visibility and "photo-op" possibilities of these types of projects. As one of the leaders of the assembly complained:

> We wanted the GAD (local government) to focus on basic needs of citizens: pollution, problems created during the rainy season, schools, health problems. They have invested in some important infrastructure projects that we also identified, and we made some progress there, but the main priorities are still unmet and when we try to push by exercising our rights to participate, local governments treat us like troublemakers.[7]

Municipal officials claim that they do respect the participatory process and point to the fact that completed projects were in fact based on the Tarqui assembly's list of alternatives but argue that parish-level citizens' assemblies cannot see the bigger picture and that authorities must balance priorities. Resident participants, on the other hand, argue that the problem is the refusal of local officials to accept the participatory rights that citizens have under the new constitution. Franklin, the assembly treasurer noted:

> We have not been able to change the way in which citizens obtain access to public goods and services. There has been an effort on the part of the (national) Executive and some ministries, but this hasn't filtered down through the whole political system. Local authorities and bureaucrats don't recognize citizen participation, so they continue to make decisions without us, and as a result, many of our priorities haven't been addressed.[8]

Attempts to engage the municipality occur through the Manta Citizens' Assembly, which includes members of local assemblies from the various parishes in Manta as well as other civil society representatives.[9] The latter, according to participants, are appointed by the mayor as opposed to being elected by citizens, which is contrary to the stipulations of the enabling legislation.[10] While representatives from the local parish assemblies (including Tarqui) are selected by participants of those mechanisms, the civil society representatives are allied with the mayor. This produces a dynamic in which both deliberation and voting are controlled by the municipality as opposed to the citizens. Furthermore, unlike in the Venezuelan cases, the Tarqui assembly does not have access to specific funds allotted to participatory mechanisms, and citizen representatives do not play a role in the allocation of these funds. Rather, they must depend on funds from the municipal government once they have submitted their priorities. This clearly diminishes the powers of the local citizens' assembly and the capacity that it has to make and implement its own decisions.

San Gabriel

This citizens' assembly is distinct from the other two Ecuadorian cases in that it predates the 2010 Citizen Participation Law. First established in 2003 by a mayor who campaigned on the theme of popular participation, the assembly was in fact a model for the type of mechanism envisaged in article 56 of the new national legislation. While originally given legal status through a municipal ordinance, the assembly became regulated by this law from 2010 onward. Alternatives identified and selected through the assembly include public control and distribution of resources such as water and gas, housing improvements, and support for small agricultural businesses prevalent in the canton.[11] The assembly has also identified a number of other infrastructure projects intended to raise the quality of life of residents in this primarily rural district.

The most significant concrete outcome mentioned by the assembly's leaders and participants involves the distribution of gas. Used for cooking and heating, this was selected by residents as a priority through a participatory and deliberative process. Distribution of gas is now coordinated through the assembly, in collaboration with the municipality, according to a needs assessment carried out by residents. This has reduced the cost of this essential resource and ensured that it is distributed equitably. The assembly was applying a similar model for other basic services at the time of research. According to residents, the gas project developed under a former municipal administration (predating the 2010 law) that demonstrated a willingness to work with the citizens' assembly. These priorities were identified by residents in the assembly and then conveyed to local elected authorities and municipal departments in meetings that included both citizen and local government representatives. The assembly has also established a limited program of loans and grants for small businesses (including agribusinesses) in cooperation with the national development agency, SENPLADES. Participants argue that central government departments are more open to citizen participation than local authorities and it is preferable to work directly with state agencies when possible.

More recently, a series of potentially larger projects aimed at improving quality of life have been less successful and residents report similar problems to those observed in Manta. Despite the 2010 legislation that theoretically provides citizens' assemblies with greater recognition and more concrete powers, residents claim that resistance to citizen participation has characterized more recent relationships with the new local administration. Thus, while the citizens' assembly had put forward a number of proposals for infrastructure and access to public services projects, many have either been rejected or replaced with initiatives selected by authorities. Assembly members point out that this is possible in large part because there are no enforcement mechanisms to require officials to respect participatory rights and because citizens' assemblies are not entitled to funds but must seek support from elected officials. As one long-term participant observed:

> Our ability to participate effectively depends a lot on the local administration. We actually had a more open local government before the new law and we made more progress even without real participatory rights. Now that the law gives us such rights, it seems to have actually gone backwards. This shows how much power local authorities have and we need measures to enforce the more equal relationship we are supposed to have.[12]

Participants agreed that the transparency generated through public participation has the potential to ensure that available funds are far more likely to be dedicated to "the common good." Yet while most respondents believe they have achieved some positive gains in terms of governance and tangible outcomes such as gas distribution, they feel that achieving these goals has required residents to "fight" local officials every step of the way and believe that the outcomes are constantly in danger of being undermined by authorities who do not understand or respect the role of public participation. There is therefore a sense that any outcomes achieved are tenuous and dependant on the openness of local authorities. Residents expressed considerable frustration with what they see as the gap between participatory rights on paper, and how these are translated into practice. These sentiments are reflected in the following statement made by one of the assembly leaders:

> Participation is established as the Fifth Power (in the Constitution) but there is no real support for these processes. When we demand what is written on paper, there is confrontation with authorities who still work in the framework of representative, delegative democracy. We have created a number of mechanisms that have a lot of potential but not many things are being practiced. The authorities do not want to understand. We need to get the local authorities to actually read the laws on citizen participation.[13]

Llano Chico

This local assembly represents a part of that parish that was recently settled. Various needs and alternatives were identified by participants but there was little consensus among participants as to what the priorities should be. Infrastructure and transportation was considered important by some, while others preferred beautification projects and building community facilities.[14] One of the most divisive issues was related to obtaining deeds for land. Some residents have sought to obtain legal ownership of land they have established their homes on (mostly indigenous families and single women) and hoped that the participatory process engendered by the existence of a citizens' assembly would help them meet these goals, while other residents participating in the same assembly claimed ownership of large parcels of land.

The assembly has produced few meaningful outcomes. There has been little progress with respect to obtaining land titles. A number of residents, primarily indigenous women, claim to have paid the landowner to purchase the lots their homes were built on but insist that they were not provided with the titles. Funding for improving housing has been distributed unevenly. Obtaining funding for housing improvement projects requires proof of home ownership and the assembly has not made an effort to help fellow participants to obtain these documents or the funding.

The only significant project completed involves the building of a community center in a part of the neighborhood characterized by more established residences. Transportation, a need identified by many of the women who work as domestic workers and must travel daily to wealthier parts of Quito, is still lacking. Only a single street had been paved, which makes access difficult. Residents must walk long distances (through muddy streets during rainy periods) to access bus routes. Basic infrastructure is still lacking in parts of the area and services have not been extended to most of the homes that require them. The poorest residents do not have water in their homes and streets remained unpaved and unlit. Utilities are localized and in private hands, contrary to the wishes of residents who hoped for public municipal utilities to be extended to their homes. Much of the land on which the neighborhood was built belongs to one individual (himself a member of the assembly) who charges residents who wish to be connected to these services; those who cannot afford installation (or choose not to pay it because they believe the municipality should do so) remain without utilities. According to residents, a number of "foreign" engineers were invited to the neighborhood by the assembly in 2012 in order to develop infrastructure projects, but these had not come to fruition at the time of a follow-up visit in July 2014.

The process of decision making observed in this assembly is characterized by conflict and exclusion, although in contrast to the two other Ecuadorian cases, these struggles tend to take place within the participatory mechanism itself and not between the assembly and local authorities. While regular sessions are held and all residents may participate, there is considerable disagreement with respect to how these function. The indigenous residents interviewed unanimously agreed that their interventions are ignored or mocked and that a handful of individuals dictate assembly decisions in a paternalistic manner. Meetings tend to proceed in a similar manner: residents are told by the assembly president about alternatives that have been selected as priorities. Some discussion takes place following the presentation of projects, although participants (particularly indigenous members) insist that this is strictly controlled by the (*mestizo*) assembly leaders and that contrary opinions are dismissed. The council's leaders deny this, arguing that all residents' opinions are heard and taken into consideration but that they must rely on technical and financial information in order to make sound decisions and present well-conceived plans to the municipal authorities. Participants were unable to provide information on what happens beyond the assembly meetings themselves. The council's leaders, meanwhile, claim that they are continuing to work on obtaining funding for the infrastructure projects mentioned above.

Not surprisingly, the majority of participants are not satisfied with either the outcomes or the process. Most suggested that while many promises were made regarding various infrastructure projects, they have seen no results other than a single paved road and that in any case, most members were not involved in the development of community priorities. Most attribute these failures to the undemocratic nature of the citizens' assembly. Typical of the sentiments expressed, an indigenous domestic worker stated that:

> In the assembly . . . the president has the last word, never the members. If we suggest 'can we do things this way?' he'll say 'no, we are doing things the way I said, I have experience and I know what is best.' I'm pretty sure this isn't what participatory democracy is supposed to be.[15]

The Llano Chico case therefore demonstrates the possibility that entrenched power relations may be reproduced within mechanisms designed to foster more inclusive deliberation and decision making. Yet the individuals who expressed disappointment with the process were not entirely discouraged. Most believed that while their experience has not been positive, they have gained experience in public speaking and (paradoxically) feel more confident about expressing themselves than in the past. All of these individuals also expressed a continued belief in the principles of participatory democracy, attributing their negative experiences to corrupt officials or racist attitudes rather than to a failure of participatory democracy per se.

Characteristics of Local Citizens' Assemblies: Understanding Why They Fall Short

The experiences of citizens who have participated in Ecuadorian local citizen assemblies supports the arguments developed in the previous chapter. They demonstrate the importance of the key characteristics identified in this book in understanding why some cases are more successful than others. In contrast to the Venezuelan cases, Ecuadorian local citizen assemblies have so far produced less satisfactory outcomes and also fare poorly with respect to autonomy, quality of deliberation, levels of participation, and (to a certain extent) inclusiveness. While good working relationships with local government could perhaps serve to strengthen the position of the assemblies, these cases reveal relationships that are often conflictual.

Autonomy and Devolution of Powers

Individuals charged with promoting the Ecuadorian government's participatory democracy agenda maintained a discourse reminiscent of the "radical" model found in Venezuela and invariably blamed local governments for the failure of this vision to be implemented. The Deputy Minister for Citizen Participation insisted that the constitution and subsequent legislation have reconfigured the relationship between citizens and the state. The "Citizen's Revolution," she claims, institutes a "new model of doing politics" in which citizens now play a leading role, in contrast to past practice, according to which citizen participation was limited to activities such as voting.[16] A senior official with the state planning and development agency (SEN-PLADES) concurs, stating that public participation is now integral to the development of public policy in Ecuador and that her department takes this very seriously.[17] Both claimed, however, that local governments (provincial and municipal) have resisted citizen participation and have implemented participatory mechanisms unenthusiastically. Citizen Participation Council (CPCCS) officials charged with regional promotion of participatory policy explained that more work needed to be done to educate local officials about citizen participation, arguing that many believe that holding a community meeting is sufficient. They stressed that participation must be active and that citizens must know (and local authorities must accept) that communities have the right to demand to be included in the policy process.

Representatives of central state agencies also argue that they attempted to give participatory mechanisms joint powers to implement projects collaboratively with local governments. Assemblies can appoint citizen representatives to work with elected officials and representatives of public or private companies to implement projects, co-manage public services or discuss development plans, public policies, and budgets. All of this should in theory provide people with a role in implementation and evaluation. Officials admit that the result has been uneven: some local assemblies actively involved in project management while others have not achieved this goal, either due to resistance from local authorities or because citizens themselves are unable or unwilling to take on this role.

Yet while their conceptualization of citizen participation is in some ways similar to that of their Venezuelan counterparts, the design and functioning of participatory mechanisms as described by Ecuadorian officials differs. It is depicted as a process in which public participation is but one aspect of the policy process and is shared with elected authorities and local government departments. First, officials stressed that public participation must follow the guidelines established by the government. As the Deputy Minister for Citizen Participation explained, citizens are supposed to decide through participatory mechanisms what the priorities should be in a given locality, but priorities have to comply with the National Plan for the Quality of Life (*Buen Vivir*). CPCCS participation specialists stated that while citizen participation is an evolving process, the current reality with respect to citizens' assemblies is that they have an "indirect" power to make decisions but they can participate in a more effective manner and can hold public officials accountable for decisions when they are familiar with the projects, the budget, and the resources available.

The mechanics of participation, then, appear to deviate somewhat from the overreaching Citizens' Revolution discourse in that "people's power" gives legitimacy to rather than replacing representatives. While the higher-level discourse is framed as "radical" democracy in terms of devolution of decision making and project implementation, the day-to-day working of participatory mechanisms does not grant citizens the extensive decision-making and implementation powers that their Venezuelan counterparts enjoy. Government officials do not always recognize the discrepancy between the higher-level discourse and the model as it has been designed in practice.

Local municipal officials do not engage in the "radical" democracy discourse observed among state officials. Both elected representatives and municipal bureaucrats understand participation as a consultative process through which they may solicit community feedback for more informed decision making and provide information to citizens about projects and budget matters. They contend, however, that it is their role to make final decisions and they must do so based on overall needs of the city and available resources, something which citizens do not understand. A municipal councillor from Manta argued that the municipality has been very open to citizen participation, dutifully setting up the citywide Citizens' Assembly to allow parish assemblies to have their say and investing considerable sums of money to improve the quality of life in lower-income districts. But, she added:

> They (local citizen assembly leaders) don't see the bigger picture, they just make demands and expect us to comply and if we

don't, some individuals believe we are not respecting their right
to participate. But we have an entire city to think about, we
have a limited budget. We want and listen to citizen feedback
but we must also plan carefully. If all the power were trans-
ferred to groups of citizens, who would do this, who would
be worrying about the bigger picture?[18]

Direct devolution of decision-making and implementation power
is not observable in any of the Ecuadorian cases. While local authorities
cannot intervene in the internal deliberation process of the local assemblies themselves, these mechanisms differ from the Venezuelan model in
that participants must work with (and often convince and pressure local
authorities) in order to have their projects implemented and adopted.
They claim that state institutions make final decisions on approved
projects, although in two of the cases (Tarqui and San Gabriel), citizens
believed that their participatory mechanism can have a limited influence
on decisions about local projects. Participants are generally aware of the
gap between what is on paper and what happens in practice. Typical of
the sentiments expressed are the following statements by local assembly
participants in San Gabriel:

The problem is that we now have all of these participatory
mechanisms such as the assemblies, which is good, but they
aren't taken seriously by local authorities who still have final
decision-making power and the resources. So we can all decide
on something here but they may still say no. What we need is
decision-making power, resources and the institutionalization
of participation so that they can't just say no.[19]

The same themes emerged among nearly all of the respondents
interviewed: they believe that they have made progress with respect to
citizen participation (which they view as democratic deepening) through
participatory mechanisms but at the same time insist that what is on paper
is not being respected in practice. Yet most respondents were optimistic
that this would evolve in time. One of the council leaders expressed:

It is a process that must continue to develop. But we are
much more developed with respect to participation than most
countries in Latin America. So we're not going to back down,

but those in power will always try to protect their interests. We have not fully used the tool that is participation yet, but we know we have the tool as a right and we will learn to use it in time whether they like it or not. I think that in another four years or so, it will be stronger.[20]

Most also mentioned the lack of directly controlled funding and the need to request financial support from municipal or central government agencies. This involves either meeting with municipal officials to present requests for specific projects or identifying national programs aimed at specific goals (such as infrastructure) and applying for funds. Participatory mechanisms are required to meet the criteria of the funding agencies and have little control over the money.

A member of the executive from the citizen's assembly in San Gabriel expressed this frequent point succinctly:

It is one thing to say that participation is important on paper, and governments are doing that more and more. But doing anything requires money and it is all an illusion unless we have access to funds so that we can implement our decisions without having to rely on always pressuring the municipalities or going through the bureaucracy of the state programs.[21]

Of the three cases studied in Ecuador, Tarqui demonstrates the most significant outcomes (hard and soft) and while the relationship with municipal officials remains conflictual, it is more productive than the other two Ecuadorian cases in that the assembly sends representatives to municipal-level mechanisms that integrate citizen representatives and decision makers. Devolution of power has barely moved beyond the consultation and participant observation stage, yet both participants and municipal officials agree that citizen participation has had an impact. While participants continue to perceive citizen participation in different terms, to some extent residents are able to use participatory mechanisms to engage with local officials to get what they want.

San Gabriel was marked by considerable conflict between elected officials and participants at the time this research was conducted. While previous municipal governments actively promoted participation, more recent officials have resisted. Most residents claimed that the current municipal government does not listen and linked the recent lack of progress to this factor. Participants pointed out, however, that successful outcomes were achieved under the past administration which was open to participation. At the time of writing, the poor relationship observed between local assembly and municipal officials had deteriorated even further, and both sides were engaged in a battle over citizens' participatory rights and funds that the assembly believes it should control. Council leaders acknowledged that no further outcomes had been achieved due to this stalemate. The Llano Chico case is marked by conflict within the local assembly itself as well as between participants and the parish administration (*administración zonal*) but closely resembles the San Gabriel case in that relationships between all parties have deteriorated to the extent that no progress is being made.

Overall, then, there is a complex relationship between devolution of powers and outcomes. The conflict observed in these cases confirms the importance of establishing effective working relationships between participatory mechanisms and authorities. Where those relationships work well and local officials are open to the value of participation (as occasionally happened in Tarqui or under past municipal administrations in San Gabriel), participants are able to play an indirect decision-making role even though such powers have not been formally devolved to neighborhood councils. The ability to play such a role also allows participants more of a say in how funding is distributed, an important factor given that participatory mechanisms lack the autonomous funding to which their Venezuelan counterparts have access.

Deliberation

Like their Venezuelan counterparts, Ecuadorian citizens' assemblies are designed to provide an environment for deliberation. Representatives interviewed from the agencies charged with supporting and promoting citizen participation focused heavily on this factor as an essential ingredient of participatory democracy. CPCCS participation advisors claimed that they support this through facilitating early meetings of newly established participatory mechanisms and offering training for how to conduct deliberative meetings (including training on how to facilitate meetings and ensure everyone is included). Participation specialists attend local citizens' assembly meetings in their assigned provinces and have observed that some individuals naturally are inclined to attempt to dominate the conversations and that those who are better educated, more articulate, or more knowledgeable about politics are more likely to impose their views by convincing others. They insist that they are working with the assemblies, however, to "teach deliberative skills" which involves ensuring that everyone's perspective is given equal weight. These officials all agree, however, that they have seen progress made in some (if not all) of the cases and that many Ecuadorians are experiencing genuine deliberation over local public policy that they have never had with representative institutions.

Citizen participants were lukewarm with respect to the internal workings of their citizens' assemblies. Only half of those interviewed believed that their local assembly provides a deliberative forum characterized by an open discussion process and that individuals who wish to speak may do so and are listened to when expressing their opinion. Fewer feel that the active members (as opposed to leaders) are the ones who participate in the elaboration of community projects within the assembly. A majority also believe that some individuals tend to dominate the discussions at least some of the time. Still, respondents tend to compare their experience in the local assembly with past attempts to be heard by municipal councils or other "traditional" government departments. Among those who were satisfied with the internal workings of their assembly, most described a process in which people are able to discuss and work with their neighbors in an egalitarian setting. They attribute "real deliberation" to the absence of hierarchies found in so many other political institutions and groups, often arguing that in dealing with any of the formal institutions, people are made aware of their place, which makes the participatory mechanisms a refreshing change.

A homemaker who had attempted various times to speak to municipal officials about paving her street noted:

> In the assembly, we can present common problems and debate with our neighbours about how best to solve them. People are people, so yes some will try to push their own interests or to dominate but at least in the citizens' assemblies we can push back, deliberation is a required part of the procedure and nobody can simply dismiss us.[22]

She went on to recall being dismissed or asked to wait indefinitely by municipal officials in the past when there was no forum for deliberation that the assemblies offer. Not surprisingly, given what we have seen about the Ecuadorian cases, there is considerable variation between the three, with the poorest outcome case (Llano Chico) faring poorly with respect to the quality of deliberation.

Participants from the Llano Chico case, with its indigenous minority population, were more likely to attribute the lack of meaningful deliberation to racism and paternalism. Of the nine cases studied, this one demonstrates the poorest tangible outcomes and spillover effects and the most negative responses with respect to deliberation (as well as the lowest-value outcomes). Most of the participants felt that the internal process was not deliberative and this includes all of the indigenous participants. They distinguished between the indigenous and *mestizo* participants, claiming that indigenous people were not taken seriously and not listened to. These individuals stated that they had hoped this attitude, so prevalent in Ecuadorian society, would not be reproduced within institutions intended to be more inclusive and deliberative. Salomé, an indigenous woman and domestic worker who had migrated from her rural home to the outskirts of Quito in search of regular employment stated:

> The local assembly is dominated by those who already have power in the community, like those who own the lots. These individuals are more educated and often take advantage of this to get their way. They tell us that they know best and the rest of us should follow, like children.[23]

The other two cases reveal somewhat more positive attitudes with around half of participants agreeing that their assembly provides a deliberative and respectful environment irrespective of local authorities' willingness to recognize the participatory mechanisms. Many participants agreed with Rusiadel, a citizen participant from Manta who observed that:

> Municipal authorities aren't listening to us, but the citizens' assemblies have rules; there is a deliberative process that has to be followed and everyone can speak and be listened to. There is a process that helps us to take what has been said and try to form a consensus. Even if municipal authorities don't want to follow up on our decisions, the deliberation gives us legitimacy, it allows us to at least pressure them because we know we have decided things in a reasonable way.

Inclusiveness

As with the other two factors, the discourse produced by the Ecuadorian state resembles that observed in Venezuela. The discursive patterns found in Ecuador generally focus on socioeconomic inclusion but also associate inclusiveness with interculturalism, including indigenous peoples and Afro-Ecuadorians. This concern for minority rights is reflected throughout the documents produced by relevant agencies such as the CPCCS, as considerable emphasis is placed on inclusivity, insisting that including everyone in society is necessary to achieve the common good. In addition to women and minority ethnic groups, Ecuadorian materials tend to be even more inclusive than those in Venezuela, often referring to, for example, LGBTQ citizens.[24]

Officials from the relevant state agencies specifically mentioned including traditionally marginalized sectors as the most important goal of participatory mechanisms. The Deputy Minister for Citizen Participation insisted that "for the first time, women are able to play a leading role in decision-making through the participatory system that, because it is new and developed in part by women, is free of some of the structural barriers found in the traditional institutions."[25] Still, these officials expressed concern about the lack of participation from certain underrepresented sectors, citing low engagement from youth and ethnic minorities in regions where they are underrepresented. They tended to attribute this to a variety of factors, including a lack of "culture of participation" and the distance required for travel to attend meetings. The Director of Citizen Initiatives conceded that racism and other forms of discrimination would continue to act as a barrier to a fully inclusive system, but insisted that his and other departments are working to break down these barriers by training these sectors on "how to participate in politics" and through helping them to build these new participatory mechanisms to provide new access points.[26]

The three local assemblies are somewhat inclusive in that they have opened participation to individuals who had never before engaged in politics other than through voting. Over half of respondents (56%) were women. The assemblies are less likely to see participation from the poorest sectors than Venezuelan communal councils, yet the largest number of respondents (20%) can be identified as precarious/unskilled workers (generally in the informal sector). Only 8% can be classified as professional (compared to 3% in Venezuela and 16% in Chile). In terms of income, a majority (59%) earned the minimum wage or less ($318 US per month at the time of research). While some respondents in Ecuador were concerned about exclusion based on political loyalties, this did not emerge as a prominent theme as it did in Venezuela. A majority of the participants interviewed felt that these mechanisms provide an expanded role to the poor in decision making, with most believing they were inclusive of those with little formal education and that they leverage the experience and abilities of all citizens.

Among those who reported positive impressions with respect to inclusiveness, many respondents pointed to the relatively closed traditional political structures dominated by "the same people" or the "same old families." Others argued that while the assemblies lack the resources they require to fully assume their roles as decision-making bodies, the fact that the poor, or those who have no connections to the political system, have a forum to express themselves is an important step in the development of democracy in Ecuador. As Betty, a homemaker and participant from the Tarqui case, mentioned:

> Those of us who don't have money or connections need a place to start if we want to exercise our rights. Trying to get into the usual government institutions is hard for those of us from humble background, so yes I think these assemblies have had a positive impact in that sense. I think we all feel much more comfortable joining organizations now that we have this knowledge, we can discuss laws at the same level as more educated people, we don't have to feel intimidated because we now have this knowledge. That makes participation so much easier and will lead to more inclusive politics.[27]

The evidence does suggest that participatory institutions in Ecuador are inclusive with respect to women. Women interviewed believed that participatory mechanisms have given them a voice that they have not experienced before. Responses reflected those provided by Venezuelan women; many contrasted local assemblies with male-dominated representative institutions. Typical of the sentiments expressed is a comment made by Miriam, a local assembly participant from Llano Chico:

> In the local and neighbourhood assemblies, there are a lot of women and many of the leaders are women, the more formal

representative institutions are always dominated by men who treat us like children. Maybe because women care more about local issues, but now I participate with my friends and even bring my daughters, we all feel we have a voice in these places because we can speak our minds.[28]

While people from marginalized sectors may be participating, they are not always listened to. Indigenous citizens in particular do not necessarily feel welcomed or respected by their non-indigenous neighbors. Of the respondents interviewed who identify as indigenous, few believed that the local citizens' assemblies are truly inclusive. They felt that the same racist attitudes they must confront in everyday life are reproduced within the assembly, which they described as yet another form of exclusion. Furthermore, in cases that are more geographically isolated many individuals who live farther from the central areas are unable to participate. As one woman expressed: "I want to attend the meetings and be part of improving my community, but here things are very spread out and we don't have a car. The assembly meets in the town; that would be an hour's walk and we don't have the time for that."[29]

Interestingly, however, many of these individuals expressed sentiments similar to those of lower-income *mestizos* in that they believed that participation in these mechanisms was helping them to gain confidence and knowledge that would lead them to a more inclusive political environment in the future. The same indigenous women who claimed that they were treated like children when asked about the deliberative quality of their local assembly asserted that while they were intimidated to speak at the earliest meetings, the experience of participation had given them the confidence they require to speak out. They tended to aware of and to emphasize the rights they have on paper and believed that they must continue to claim these rights.

Levels of Participation

Ecuadorian state officials agree that there is not enough citizen engagement and that this has a negative impact on the ability of councils to produce positive outcomes. The government estimates that less than 10% of the population has been involved in one of the new participatory mechanisms and believes that more significant outcomes will continue to lag unless it can encourage more people to engage. The general consensus among state officials and observers is that mass participation did not work in the Ecuadorian Citizen's Revolution as it did with Venezuela's Bolivarian Revolution. Some attribute this to political culture; Ecuadorians are accustomed to spontaneous and cyclical participation in times of economic or political crisis which has led to the extra-institutional replacement of governments. The type of social organization prevalent prior to the current government's "Citizens' Revolution" agenda reflects these patterns and translates into a lack of experience with sustained, institutionalized forms of organization. Others point to "participation fatigue" after years of uprisings and unstable governments and the weakening of social movements that has occurred through cooptation following Correa's election in 2007. Furthermore, the economy has seen sustained growth along with unprecedented improvements in socioeconomic conditions and more social spending than any other government in the country's history. The quality of life has improved for many and this has occurred simultaneously with the expansion of participatory mechanisms, making participation less necessary for many, because material conditions have already improved due to top-down redistribution. This aligns with the perception expressed by government agents and active participants who felt that people tend to view participation as a means of achieving immediate material benefits and do not subscribe to a broader participatory democracy agenda.

Participation has been relatively low across the three cases. Because the assemblies operate at the parish level (a larger unit than the neighborhoods represented by participatory mechanisms in Venezuela and Chile), it is more difficult to determine numbers of potential members. While in the other two countries councils have boundaries defined by local streets and are able to produce figures on how many families live within the delineated area, the potential pool or participants in Ecuador is assumed to be the parish. Available information for the three cases reveals that less than 10% of residents represented by the Tarqui local assembly have participated at some time, while this number drops to less than 5% in the other cases.[30]

State agencies are making an effort to encourage participation through promotional campaigns and delivering workshops. CPCCS agents engage in awareness campaigns with the public to educate them about participatory rights and how to form a local citizens' assembly. In many cases, this leads to the creating of a "founding group" of citizens whose role is to motivate others to join, ideally seeking out broad representation in their efforts to form an assembly (ethic groups, women). They are provided with training and support until the assembly is constituted. Yet in many case, only members of the directive participate with any regularity, meaning that broad participation is lacking. Participants and state representatives identified numerous obstacles. These include time constraints and family responsibilities, the complex and time-intensive nature of institutionalized participation, low levels of interpersonal trust, and lack of interest. As one directive member argued, "these barriers can be overcome for a time when people have a pressing need, but the momentum soon dissipates."[31] Others suggest that while there is an array of participatory rights on paper, citizens are not well informed with respect to how to use them to engage with this complex system. The importance of results and outcomes is also addressed as a factor that determines levels of participation. Blanca, who served as secretary of her local assembly, identified many of her peers' frustrations:

> When people see that participation is making a difference, they will be more inclined to participate, but people are often not patient. This creates a negative cycle: when they do not see results right away, they stop participating, which in turn harms the capacity of the assembly to produce outcomes.[32]

These observations likely explain in part the lack of participation in Ecuador and are also supported by the relatively sustained rates of participation in Venezuela, where cases have also experienced more significant results.

There is also a noticeable lack of interest and reluctance to participate on the part of young people; in all three cases less than 5% of citizen participants are under 30 years of age. Those who do participate are said to be always the same people; some respondents used the term "career participatory citizens" which defeats the purpose. Some council leaders and more active participants describe a freeloader effect when discussing the nature of participation they have observed and argue many participants themselves do not respect the participatory process. Here, they refer to individuals who only participate sporadically—when they want something—and whose participation is only aimed at securing personal benefits for their families, which does not help the process.

State-Society Relationships

Not surprisingly, the spillover effects observed in the three Ecuadorian cases are less positive than in Venezuela. Compared with their Venezuelan counterparts, fewer respondents from Ecuador's local citizen assemblies are either satisfied or very satisfied with the quality of participation in their country; over half cited that participatory rights are not being fully respected by all levels of government or that there is a gap between what is on paper and how things work in practice.

Still, most are hopeful that something has been unleashed that cannot be put back in the bottle and that participatory rights will evolve with time. This perspective appears to be influenced by two factors. First, while we have seen that participation in practice does not always meet the expectations created by central government discourse, participants emphasized the importance of the constitutional and legislative changes providing more "radical" democracy. Most believed that regardless of how well things are currently working in practice, having achieved "on paper" rights is a victory for participatory democracy, arguing that citizens must first have rights in order to exercise them. They express optimism that deficiencies will be corrected. Many respondents spoke in the future tense with respect to seeing the results of participatory democracy and pointed out that it is impossible to transition from a system of representative to participatory democracy in less than a decade and that a full transformation will require far more time and will likely involve many mistakes. As one respondent from San Gabriel stated:

> Our representative institutions have been around for almost 200 years and they still don't work, nobody can expect to build a perfectly functioning participatory democracy in ten years.[33]

José, a member of his local citizen council's directive who has been struggling to position the mechanism to play a greater role in decision making insisted:

> Knowing what our rights are is the first step, you can't claim rights that you don't know you have. I think we all feel much more comfortable joining organizations now that we have this knowledge, we can discuss laws at the same level as more educated people, we don't have to feel intimidated because we

have this knowledge, that makes participation so much easier and will ultimately make democracy stronger.[34]

Many participants also view participation as a good in itself, often relating this to skills acquisition, knowledge, and confidence. One of the most common assertions revolved around themes of democratic learning, competence, and self-confidence gained through participation in the public sphere. Some attributed their new knowledge directly to the experience of participation. As Miriam, a domestic worker who has been critical of her experience participating in the local citizens' assembly, said:

> At first, it was difficult (to participate) because I didn't know anything about how things work or even what my own rights were. After spending a few months participating in the assembly, I started to know a lot about the constitution, about laws. I started to feel more confident about myself, so this has helped my personal development even if we have not yet seen the benefits we are hoping for.[35]

As in Venezuela, it appears that party affiliation is a factor with respect to empowerment and positive perceptions of democracy. Controlling for this variable, it is clear that participants who do not identify strongly with the party in power (Alianza PAIS) are less inclined to hold the favorable views expressed in the broader sample. Less than half of non-AP aligned Ecuadorian subjects agree that they are satisfied or very satisfied with democracy in their country. The percentage of respondents who support this view rises to 60% when only looking at government supporters.

There is a close alignment between citizens' perceptions and the "radical democracy" discourse of President Correa and state institutions. Democracy itself is conceived of in terms of its variants. References to democracy are preceded or followed by qualifiers such as "participatory," "real," "social," and "popular" on the one hand or "representative," "past," "false," and "elite" on the other. The former terms are associated with the ability of citizens to exercise agency, while the latter are linked discursively to passive citizenship and exclusion. The citizen was most frequently framed in collective terms and linked discursively to participation, dignity, and equality. The perspective of a school teacher from Manta is typical of respondents who engaged with these concepts:

Being a citizen means having dignity and being treated with dignity. This is different from just voting in elections. And dignity requires a certain level of equality. People cannot really exercise their participatory rights if there are such inequalities that prevent them from participating on equal terms. They (the opposition) don't want us to be citizens, they just want us to be consumers.[36]

Representatives, particularly those at the local level or members of the legislature, are not seen as legitimate. Much of the discourse assumes the representation is a farce and that citizenship can only be achieved through participation, as exemplified in the following statement offered by a participant from the Tarqui assembly:

Those who get elected cannot represent citizens. They represent themselves, they represent their parties, they represent those that give them funding and support, they don't represent us citizens. Only we can represent ourselves by participating in the process (of decision-making), by demanding that these rights be recognized.[37]

The only references to voting in the context of elections for representative institutions (municipal government or the National Assembly) tend to arise in a negative context, as in the following example provided by a domestic worker from the outskirts of Quito:

Voting for *asambleístas* (elected members of the legislature) or for municipal councillors, what does that do for the people? Once elected, they forget we exist and serve their own interests. We are tired of that, citizen participation and participatory institutions have legitimacy, we just need to make sure they (the representatives) accept and recognize that.[38]

As in Venezuela, these conceptions of democracy closely mirror the discursive patterns found both in legislation and participatory training materials and suggest some level of influence, especially among supporters of Correa and his party. Another striking similarity is that participation is associated with local assemblies or other mechanisms established by the Citizen Participation Law. This has the potential to exclude other organizations, including some of these countries' most historically dynamic organizations, such as indigenous social movement groups. Some observers argue that diversity and inclusion are on the agenda now and these things were not spoken of before, but the concern is that it has all been institutionalized into the state, whereas it used to happen outside of the state. They contend that the groups that represent various interests (indigenous, women's) are in fact becoming weaker because of this; they are being overshadowed by state institutions. While there is more inclusion, this inclusion may be controlled. Yet another parallel between the two countries involves the scope of participation that is "available" for public participation. Like communal councils, local citizen assemblies are focused on local needs such as improved infrastructure and social development, and their influence (such as it may be) can rarely extend beyond the community. Questions of national importance remain within the purview of central government agencies.

Conclusions

The tangible outcomes observed in the Ecuadorian cases are relatively modest in comparison with those seen in Venezuela. Despite the "citizens' power" state discourse, the participatory mechanisms do not fare well with respect to the key characteristics identified in the participatory democracy literature (see summary in table 5.2). Participation has been expanded to some traditionally disadvantaged groups (the poor, women). People who would not normally have had any access to decision making can have some say by using assemblies to exert pressure; this is more effective than trying to do so individually. Certain individuals and groups tend to dominate, however, and indigenous citizens continue to feel excluded. Local citizen assemblies do not demonstrate a real devolution of decision making to citizens and participants have been only moderately successful in using participatory mechanisms to get what they want through working with or pressuring local authorities.

Venezuelan communal council participants used the powers available to them to translate their decisions into practice but relationships between citizen assembly participants in Ecuador and local officials are often marked by conflict. Authorities resist public participation and citizens are not satisfied with the participatory process and express hostility toward local officials. This tension is related to the gap between their expectations and

Table 5.2. Projects, Processes, and Outcomes, Ecuador

	Alternatives Selected	Process	Outcomes
Tarqui	• Construction of streets and sidewalks • Construction and beautification of parks and public spaces • Updating the water system • Clean up pollution in the 2 rivers that cross the parish • Structural improvements to schools in poor condition	Participants identify needs and select priorities Authorities make final decisions	Medium-Low value • Construction or re-construction of streets and sidewalks • Updating of water system in parts • Community center • Beautification projects for parks
San Gabriel	• More equitable distribution of essential resources such as gas and water • Identifying needs for the purposes of targeting social spending • Support for small businesses • Housing improvements • Extension of utilities to areas not covered	Citizens play no role in obtaining funding Implementation carried out by state agencies Relationship with authorities characterized by conflict	Low value • Distribution of gas through the assembly • Small development funds for small and medium businesses
Llano Chico	• Lack of public services for many homes: water, sanitation, electricity • Streets not paved • Access to public transportation • Community facilities: medical facilities, sports facilities, etc. • Families require deeds for their land		Low value • Community center built • One street paved

reality. Having internalized the central government's discourse, which is similar in nature to Venezuela, participants are aware of their "on paper" rights and expect to be able to exercise them. This message has not been embraced by local level politicians and bureaucrats, who see decision making and implementation as their responsibility and view participation as primarily consultative.

When participants expect radical democracy but must work through mechanisms that do not provide such powers, these relationships become conflictual, which then results in participants being left out of an informal or "observer" role. The association between key characteristics (lack of participation and the related problems with internal deliberation and inclusiveness) and the poor outcomes produced by these cases confirms the importance of positive relationships between participatory mechanisms and local government when formal decision-making and implementation powers are lacking.

6

Chile

Pragmatic Citizen Participation

Chile is praised by some observers for the strength of its representative institutions in a region where liberal democracy has been weak, but citizen participation beyond elections has been limited and often discouraged by the state. While the *juntas de vecinos* (neighborhood councils) have existed for decades, citizen participation has only recently emerged as part of the mainstream political discourse, accompanied by new legislation and mechanisms. This represents a marked shift when compared to the past several decades, although the type of participation that is encouraged is relatively limited and framed as improving governance and enhancing (rather than replacing) representative democracy. For this reason, it makes sense to define the Chilean model as one of pragmatic citizen participation as opposed to radical participatory democracy.

The Chilean cases have provided residents with important outcomes despite the more constrained nature of citizen participation and the limited powers that characterize participatory mechanisms in that country. It is also clear that citizens' expectations of what their role should be as citizen participants are very different from those encountered in Venezuela and Ecuador. What is striking is that despite the lack of "radical" participatory democracy discourse and the relatively limited powers of Chilean neighborhood councils, these outcomes are at least as successful, and arguably more so, than those observed in Ecuador. Most neighborhood council leaders and participants argue that they have had an impact on their communities through participation. In all cases, residents, local officials, and available documentation suggest that participatory mechanisms did play an important role in achieving these gains although, in contrast to the Venezuelan cases, outcomes are attributed to both the efforts of participatory mechanisms and municipal governments. The councils demonstrate moderate levels of inclusiveness, quality of deliberation, and participation, with some variation between the cases. Although none have experienced significant devolution of powers, participants have managed to play a role by developing working relationships with relevant municipal actors. Venezuelan communal council participants used the powers available to them to translate their decisions into practice, while Chileans used their neighborhood councils to collaborate with (and sometimes pressure) local officials and represent collective demands. Communities can therefore use these institutions to resolve long-standing infrastructure problems that municipal governments may otherwise ignore, but they are using them in very different ways from their Venezuelan counterparts.

The Cases

The first case is situated in the 6 de Mayo neighborhood of La Pintana, the poorest of Santiago's 37 communes and one of the lowest-income urban municipalities in Chile. It is primarily residential and most businesses are small and cater to local residents. It falls below the national average with respect to various socioeconomic indicators. In 2009, about 27% of the population was considered poor, well above the average of 11.5% for Greater Santiago and the 14% national average.[1] Just over 600 individuals are registered as members of the neighborhood council and the directive is made up of four individuals. The largest number of respondents (22%) identified themselves as laborers. This category included many self-employed individuals. Other common categories include homemakers, domestic workers, and tradespeople; and a few respondents were unemployed or retired.

The second neighborhood council is located in the Villa Versalles neighborhood of Maipú, also in Greater Santiago. The largest commune by population, it is primarily middle-class and above average with respect to various socioeconomic indicators, including housing and wellness. It is primarily residential but also contains a significant variety of businesses and retail options. The neighborhood council represents about 500 families. Nearly 900 people are registered in the council's members' book, although only about 60 participate on a regular basis. The council's directive consists of only three people. There was significant variation in occupational categories: skilled laborers, professionals, office personnel, homemakers, teachers, and skilled tradespeople.

The third case is located in Cayumapú, a semi-rural district within the commune of Valdivia in Chile's southern Los Ríos region. The economy is strongly dependent on forestry, agriculture, and tourism, while the city of Valdivia is an important university town and tourist center. The commune is characterized by mixed socioeconomic indicators, but has a relatively high poverty rate. The council is relatively small as only about 170 individuals are registered as members. The employment categories of respondents are different from the other two cases and reflect the rural nature of the district. Many residents are employed in areas such as forestry and agriculture. The largest single employer produces and ships flowers; many residents are employed in activities such as packing bulbs. The second largest employer is a cheese factory. Others commute to the city of Valdivia and work as laborers or retail workers.

Outcomes

Medium-value outcomes were achieved in these cases. Compared to the Venezuelan communal councils, these projects are somewhat smaller in scope, were generally completed in a less timely manner, and resident satisfaction with both the outcomes and processes is mixed. Still, many of the alternatives proposed by neighborhood council members through their participatory process were translated into concrete outcomes and these had a positive impact on material conditions (see table 6.1).

6 de Mayo

This neighborhood council represents one of Chile's poorest urban districts but exhibits the most significant outcomes of the three Chilean cases studied. Founded in the 1970s, this council is also the oldest of the participatory mechanisms studied in this book.[2] Unlike similar neighborhoods in Venezuela, both residents and local officials insisted that the commune is covered by basic services and paved streets. Original residents claimed that when they arrived in the 1970s, the sector did not have access to drinking water or electricity. These services were installed in the late 1970s, followed

Table 6.1. Outcome Evaluation Criteria, Chile

Case	Tangible Outcomes	Alignment with Alternatives	Scope	Improvement to Quality of Life	Participants' Role in Participatory Relationship	Participants' Role Aligns with Institutional Design
6 de Mayo	Medium-High Value	Strong-Moderate	Moderate	Moderate	Subordinate, primarily cooperative	Yes
Versalles	Medium value	Strong-Moderate	Moderate	Moderate	Subordinate, primarily cooperative	Yes
Cayumapú	Medium value	Moderate	Moderate	Moderate	Subordinate,	Yes primarily cooperative

by the paving of local streets, with the participation of residents through the neighborhood council. Residents also mentioned that in these early years the council was instrumental in establishing and running community kitchens for the poorest families. For comparative purposes, research for this case focused on more recent projects for which documentation was available. The alternatives identified by residents through assemblies convened by the council's leaders included housing improvement projects, improving public lighting (a need which many linked to the area's relatively high crime rate), improving streets and sidewalks, building sports facilities, beautification projects (particularly parks), and obtaining better public transportation. The outcomes have been categorized as medium-value; they are fairly well aligned with citizens' preferred alternatives, are significant in scope, and have had a positive impact on residents' standard of living.

The most significant initiative undertaken since 2009 was a housing improvement project that has benefited over 100 families. These improvements involved not only structural upgrades such as roofing, but renovations to kitchens, bathrooms, and plumbing systems. In many cases, these upgrades allowed houses in poor condition to become "like new." Collectively, the residents received 115,000,000 CLP (just under $212,500 US at 2009 exchange rates). This amounted to about 1,150,000 CLP (just over $2,000 US) per selected family.[3] The process exhibits some similarities with initiatives in Venezuela at the earlier stages, yet it diverges from these cases with respect to the level of community involvement in decision making and (especially) implementation. Housing renovations were identified as the most pressing need by residents during a series of assemblies convened by the council's president. The council's leadership subsequently applied for funding from a housing improvement fund administered by the national Ministry of Housing and Urban Affairs (MINVU), using the community's engagement through the council to support their application for a group subsidy. All residents represented by the council were invited to apply, although selection criteria established by the MINVU require that eligible families must demonstrate a certain level of need (the ministry applies a formula to determine this).[4] Specific homes were identified in the application procedure based on these criteria. While community involvement was active during the early stages and was essential in supporting the group subsidy application, technocrats from the MINVU ultimately decided on which homes were eligible for funding and were also responsible for implementing the projects. While residents certainly were consulted with respect to what they wanted the money used for, MINVU agents oversaw all aspects of the work carried out.

A number of neighborhood infrastructure projects were also spear-headed by the council.[5] These include the construction of several sports courts and of a community gymnasium. A park was later developed in which local residents can create their own gardens, and other parks, plazas, and paths were repaired and updated. Street lighting was installed on over 30 blocks within the neighborhood. Needs were determined in a community forum during which neighbors were asked to identify the most pressing collective problems faced by their community. All residents were invited to attend and to vote on priorities based on proposals put forward by council leadership. The council then established a list of priorities and applied for funding through the *Quiero mi Barrio* (I Love My Neighbour-hood) program, an initiative of the Bachelet administration intended to contribute to improving the quality of life for residents of neighborhoods faced with deteriorating public spaces, public property, urban environments, and problems of segregation and/or vulnerability through a participatory and sustainable process. Administered by the MINVU, the program is intended to be participatory and to involve residents in the identification of priorities. While applications do not have to be channeled through a neighborhood council, this particular council did play a leading role and as a result, the neighborhood was one of a limited number in the country selected each year to benefit from the program.

Finally, the council successfully worked to improve public transportation to and from the neighborhood. Well beyond the furthest reaches of the Santiago metro system, residents complained that the neighborhood was not adequately covered by the system of small buses (micros) that operate in the less central areas of the city. The situation has been dramatically improved, with two micro lines serving the area, beginning at 5:00 a.m. as requested by locals who must travel long distances to work. Achieving this outcome involved applying pressure to the municipal government and is an interesting example of how Chile's neighborhood councils work. A series of assemblies were convened by the council's leaders during which local residents discussed transportation needs and solutions (including service routes, schedules, etc.). Using this feedback, council leaders established a "sectorial roundtable" consisting of council members, other local groups (representing the elderly, environmental issues, etc.), and officials from La Pintana's municipal transportation department. When they did not receive the desired response, leaders used the neighborhood council to seek support from, and mobilize, the population. The community responded in large numbers and this mobilization exerted sufficient pressure on the municipal office to elicit a positive response. Representatives of the roundtable met with the municipal director of transportation armed with evidence of this community support, and plans were soon drawn up (by the transportation department) to extend micro service to the neighborhood based on the proposal originally submitted by the neighborhood council.

A majority of the subjects interviewed agreed that their standard of living has improved as a result of the work of their neighborhood council. Unlike in Venezuela, requests for access to funding programs, such as the MINVU housing improvement subsidies and *Quiero mi Barrio*, are not required to be channeled through the neighborhood councils.[6] Still, residents were of the opinion that the council was instrumental in ensuring that the community received the maximum amount. Participants expressed satisfaction with the outcomes achieved and believed that the council played a key role, with most pointing to less favorable results in neighboring areas without an effective council. While the MINVU housing subsidy is offered on an individual or group basis, residents felt that their chances of obtaining funding were improved due to the collective pressure exercised through their participatory mechanism. Municipal officials also pointed to this case as a positive example of how a neighborhood council should work, although, unlike in Venezuela, they attributed the outcomes to a combination of public participation and the openness of municipal officials.

Despite a more restrained role in the overall process, participants were generally pleased with their experience. Of the four more active members and members of the directive, all insisted that they have a good relationship with the municipality and that municipal officials demonstrate an "openness" and a willingness to work with the council. Further, in contrast to the Venezuelan cases, respondents demonstrated an eagerness to work with groups outside of their participatory mechanism: leaders mentioned that they have been involved in numerous "sectoral roundtables" with organizations representing the elderly and sports associations among others.

Versalles

A primarily middle-income Santiago suburb, Mapiú is considerably more developed than La Pintana and enjoys good infrastructure and public services. The alternatives identified by residents through their neighborhood council primarily consist of housing renovations and relatively minor repairs to public goods such as street lighting, sidewalks, and parks. The outcomes are less significant in scope than in the previous case, but generally reflect the alternatives selected by participants and have had a positive impact on quality of life.

The council undertook a collective housing improvement project, although the types of renovations requested by residents were relatively minor compared with those in the poorer municipality. From 2009 to 2012, 48 families registered for, and received, funding to repair and upgrade their homes, with another 43 approved for the program at the time of research.[7] Amounts received were smaller than in the 6 de Mayo case, ranging from 60,000 to 590,000 CLP ($100 to $1,000 US). The types of repairs conducted ranged from replacing bathroom fixtures to installing new flooring. The council was also instrumental in tackling a pollution problem caused by an untreated watercourse that crosses the neighborhood. Residents complained that the stagnant water produced unpleasant odors and constituted a health concern; through the work of the council this canal was filled with concrete. Other projects successfully carried out include repairs to sidewalks, storm drains, and street lights; purchase and distribution of burglar alarms; and distribution of waste containers.

More so than in the other cases, this council has taken a role in ensuring public security in the neighborhood; the council president claimed that she and her fellow leaders have established (at the request of residents) a strong working relationship with local police and are in contact regularly.

The agenda-setting, decision-making, and implementation processes closely mirror those observed in 6 de Mayo. The council holds regular assemblies with members of the community; meetings times and locations are posted throughout the neighborhood and all residents (whether registered with the council or not) may attend, participate, and vote on matters. Some of these meetings focus on identifying and prioritizing problems while others involve proposing solutions. Proposals are generally put forward by the council's leaders based on priorities established at the previous meeting. Attendees then discuss and debate these proposals, followed by a vote, the details of which are recorded by the council's secretary. Once the vote has taken place and the council's leaders have been given a mandate to pursue a particular policy, they take this forward to the department or individual most likely to help them implement the proposals. This may be the head of the relevant municipal (or central government) department, a municipal councillor, or even the commune's mayor.

It is through this process that housing repairs were identified as the most pressing issue facing neighbors in 2009. Once the decision had been made through the council to make this a priority, the leaders identified a promising funding program, but rather than apply for funding as a group, they chose to assist families to apply for individual subsidies. Successful applicants were required to demonstrate a certain level of need based on a point system; the council played a liaison role between members and the MINVU to ensure that eligible families were identified and that successful applicants received the money. The families were free to work with MINVU officials to decide how they wanted the funds to be used. Similar to 6 de Mayo, but in contrast to the Venezuelan cases, the council's part in the administration of the housing subsidies was primarily an oversight role once the application was accepted. SERVIU (the technical service department of MINVU) oversees the projects, sending inspectors from house to house to assess the work and authorizes the release of funds. The other major community projects were primarily the result of negotiations between the council's leaders and municipal officials. Armed with decisions and voting records, leaders scheduled meetings with planning agents of the relevant departments such as Public Works and negotiated what they wanted, but final decisions would lie with the officials.

Most residents were satisfied with the outcomes and felt that the council was instrumental in achieving these outcomes. Municipal councillors and civil servants tended to describe neighborhood councils as important partners in local governance and attributed the outcomes to both the neighborhood council and a willingness of the municipality to work with citizens. They argued that they would receive essential information about community needs and preferences from these mechanisms. Those who did benefit directly from the programs (about half of the individuals interviewed) believed that their material conditions had improved as a result, although other residents felt that they had not seen a significant improvement in their standard of living.

Cayumapú

This rural community differs from the other two Chilean cases in that parts of the area lack basic services and infrastructure. The needs identified by residents reflect this relative underdevelopment: they want streets paved, lighting installed, and plumbing extended to all homes (many still do not have indoor washrooms). While the council has had some success with significant infrastructure projects, many of the desired improvements have not yet materialized. The scope of the outcomes is limited, but not insignificant for this relatively poor rural district and residents have seen a modest improvement to their standard of living.

The most important project in recent years involved bringing drinking water to the community by extending service from the city of Valdivia. This was only achieved in 2008; prior to this, residents extracted water from local wells. Drinking water is now available to 90% of residents represented by the council. The other partially successful project consisted of installing lighting in parts of the sector, although this fell well below participants' expectations. Only areas around the main square and a couple of main arteries are now illuminated. Paving residential streets was another major priority identified by residents, but at the time of research only a single central street had been paved. Finally, as in the other two Chilean cases, the council coordinated a home improvement campaign in the sector; 12 families benefited and the average amount received was 330,000 CLP (about $625 US). These families applied this to bringing basic amenities into their home, particularly installing modern bathrooms.[8]

The neighborhood council's internal process shares much in common with the other two Chilean cases. Discussion and debate takes place at regular citizens' assemblies where participants present problems and attempt to find solutions. Proposals are presented by council leaders and voted on by citizens, and these are then taken forward to the appropriate authorities. This procedure was employed for the various projects mentioned above, including public lighting and street paving, although the results have been disappointing compared to the other two Chilean cases. Local officials attribute this not to the failure of citizen participation but to the lack of funding in this relatively poor region and to logistical complexities of extending services to a rural region with a relatively dispersed population. For example, with respect to street lighting, municipal agents argued that it is simply not possible to provide the service to every street at this time but that priorities must be developed. They prefer to focus on areas where the maximum number of residents will benefit and/or on key arteries, but identifying these is time-consuming and requires careful planning, all of which creates delays.

The council differs in that it has made use of larger organizations to pursue its interests. Because councils in the region represent relatively small populations and are dispersed throughout a large area, residents have long felt that their neighborhood councils were insufficient to promote their interests and that the needs of a widespread area would be better served by uniting under larger organizations. Leaders also viewed the scope of neighborhood councils as too limited to pursue regional policy goals, such as access to water, claiming that there are restrictions with respect to what types of funds they may apply for. Thus, when neighborhood council participants decided through the discussion and debate process in the mid-2000s to make water a priority, they approached other councils in the area to establish a water committee to apply for funding to install water. From that point on, the water committee worked with the municipal technical assistance unit to prepare a strong proposal (including the number of homes to be connected to the water system, costs, and other details). The proposal was presented to decision makers from the municipal (Valdivia) and regional (XIV, Los Ríos) governments, both of which have infrastructure funds to support this type of investment. The entire process took a couple of years. Council leaders insist (and participants agree) that water committee representatives maintained strong ties to the neighborhood councils by providing regular updates at citizen assemblies.

The council has also participated in a new structure created by the 2011 Popular Participation Law. Community organizations (including neighborhood councils) may establish a Communal Council of Civil

Society Organizations (*Consejo Comunal de Organizaciones de la Sociedad Civil*, COSOC) to represent, aggregate, and pursue the interests of multiple councils or other civil society groups in a given territory. The president of the Cayumapú neighborhood council sits on the local COSCO and in this capacity is expected to represent the demands of all neighborhood councils represented by this body. His role is to present problems and proposals decided on by neighborhood councils to the municipal and regional governments. Participants hope that this new structure will enhance their ability to use pressure to achieve larger-scale goals by presenting the demands of multiple councils to local and regional decision makers.

Participants expressed mixed feelings with respect to the benefits they had achieved through their neighborhood council. Still, when asked about the projects that have been completed, most believed that community participation was essential in achieving these outcomes, with most arguing that their area would still be without water services if it were not for the pressure exerted by the neighborhood council, water committee, and other participatory mechanisms. Local officials from the municipal and regional governments agreed, although they framed their perspective differently, arguing that participatory mechanisms help them to know what the public wants and therefore to develop policy priorities.

Characteristics of Chilean Neighborhood Councils: Understanding Their Potential

In terms of inclusiveness, participation has been expanded to an extent in the context of a closed Chilean political system. Many groups remain excluded, however, and rates of sustained participation are low, although we see higher levels of inclusion in the most successful case. The councils provide a forum for deliberation in a system that has rarely elicited the input of the average citizen, but neighborhood councils do not demonstrate a real devolution of decision making to citizens. People can decide what they want in the councils, but these decisions must then be accepted by state or municipal officials if they are to be implemented. Local authorities have final say and decisions made through this process cannot be translated into action directly. Still, participants (or at least council leaders) find ways of using participation to their advantage. They can be more deeply involved in the process despite lacking decision-making and implementation powers and both they and municipal authorities value the relationship.

Devolution of Powers and Autonomy

Discourse produced by state institutions and relevant legislation establish devolution of power to citizens as the basis of the participatory democracy agenda in Venezuela and to a lesser extent in Ecuador, while in Chile it is not framed as an essential characteristic of public participation nor are participatory mechanisms designed with this goal in mind. Elected officials and civil servants in Chile almost unanimously understood participation not as involving devolution of power to the people but rather as a means of giving citizens an expanded role in the process and consulting neighbors in order to make more informed decisions. The advisor on Citizen Participation to the Minister Secretary General of Government (MSGG, the department charged with implementing participatory governance initiatives) was clear on this point, stating that the 2011 Participation Law and the participatory policy of the government are focused on "consultation and provision of information" and that participatory mechanisms "do not have decision-making powers." She insisted, however, that the government was working toward the "institutionalization of citizen participation in Chile" and, while people can be "critical with respect to the achievements thus far, it is an important first step."[9] The former director of the Social Organizations Division of the MSGG under the Bachelet administration concurred with this assessment, but argued that the law has not been implemented to its fullest extent and that the original intention was to allow citizens more involvement in the decision-making process.[10]

In contrast to the Venezuelan model, Chilean neighborhood assemblies do not have implementation powers. While the enabling legislation does state that the councils are intended to "propose and execute projects that benefit the community" representatives of the central government stressed the concept of co-management, by which they meant that council members may "observe" the implementation of projects in collaboration with state and local officials. One of the government lawyers responsible for citizen participation policy explained that the understanding of "implementation" with respect to participatory mechanisms in Chile is to ensure transparency and accountability to the community by allowing neighborhood council leaders the right to "observe."[11]

Elected officials from the La Pintana and Maipú municipal governments confirmed the consultative nature of the role of neighborhood councils and other participatory institutions, yet demonstrated a willingness to work with representatives from neighborhood councils. These individuals insisted that it is their responsibility to make decisions and use the resources with which they are entrusted, stressing that this is what they were elected to do and that they would be neglecting their responsibilities if they did not take their role seriously. However, they did stress that they value participation and consider citizen feedback valuable and beneficial to both sides. As summarized by one municipal councillor:

> Having them (neighbourhood council representatives) involved not only helps to ensure that what we do responds to community needs, but also creates a greater sense of trust between us and the community; they are able to feel that they have played some part in the decisions made and therefore are more invested in these decisions, which in turn provides our actions with more legitimacy.[12]

Individuals outside of the political system who study public participation provided a similar perspective, arguing that more significant outcomes have been observed in municipalities that are more open to participation. They stressed that outcomes (particularly spillover effects) would be further improved if participatory mechanisms were able to play a more formal decision-making and implementation role but tended to blame the Chilean political system for concentrating power in the hands of mayors at the local level, pointing out that mayors resisted any measures that would diminish their own powers.[13]

In sharp contrast to communal council participants in Venezuela, nearly all of the participants mentioned that the powers of the neighborhood councils are limited and that they must work with and develop good relationships with municipal officials if they are to have any hope of having neighbors' decisions translated into action. Unlike in Ecuador, they perceived this as natural and likely to continue. "Neighbourhood council citizen participation is understood as participation always is in Chile" says council president Pablo, echoing sentiments expressed by many interviewees. "It doesn't establish any real power or autonomy from government, it is consultative and discretionary." [14] Gloria, president of the 6 de Mayo case, elaborates that:

> Within the council itself, there is decision-making, neighbours discuss things and vote on them. That can be very positive. But we then have to convince the municipality to accept our decisions; this takes a lot of work and putting pressure on them.[15]

Citizen participants have limited expectations with respect to what powers their mechanisms should have. They do not understand them as replacing representative democracy but rather view the role of participation as gathering feedback from community members and transmitting this feedback to elected officials. This is not to say that Chilean neighborhood councils are entirely passive; they clearly believe that decisions made through the participatory process have more legitimacy than those made by officials alone. They also believe that this gives them the right to use participatory mechanisms to pressure elected officials to implement neighborhood council decisions. As one president put it, "if one official turns down a request that has been backed by the neighborhood council, they will go above that person's head to seek a more sympathetic ear," a strategy which has occasionally taken them as far as the mayor's office. This perspective can be observed in all three cases and the relative success of these mechanisms at generating tangible outcomes requires us to reconsider the role of autonomy and devolution in achieving outcomes. Council president Pablo summarized this in the following manner:

> But we have tools we can use to pressure them (protests, local media). And so we put pressure on the mayor and councillors and they know that if they do not want to have problems, they will do what the community has asked for through the councils. Because we are the base, we represent the needs of the people.[16]

The 6 de Mayo council president elaborated further:

> We demand respect. We have talked to people from all levels of government who come here with their fancy discourse but we tell them that we don't want to hear these words, we want results. That just because we are not highly educated doesn't mean we don't think. Life has taught us much, we know what our community's needs are and we expect to have some say. So, we will work with them but in a relationship of mutual respect.[17]

However, the most effective outcomes are produced when council participants develop and maintain strong relationships based on mutual trust and respect with local officials. By using their mechanisms in these ways, they are able to achieve important outcomes despite the lack of real decision-making powers.

Although fewer participants were able to describe the details of the participatory process in comparison to the Venezuelan respondents, the process described is similar across the Chilean cases. Needs are determined in a community forum during which neighbors are asked to identify problems and alternatives. All residents vote based on proposals put forward by council leadership. The council then establishes a list of priorities and leaders take these demands to relevant officials (elected or municipal department heads) and/or apply for funding through the most appropriate government programs. Participants were thus able to play at least a limited role in decision making and implementation through an indirect role in the decision-making process even when such power has not been formally devolved. They were also generally able to "monitor" the implementation of projects. They are able to play this role by establishing effective relationships with relevant authorities or by engaging in mechanisms that interface with local government. The president of the Cayumapú neighborhood council further elaborates:

> The law says they have to consult us, it doesn't say they have to adopt our decisions. I can't say I have any decision-making powers, but I do have the right to be consulted and the obligation to represent my community in presenting their needs to the municipality. By developing relationships with the appropriate people, we can also monitor implementation and are involved in evaluating results.[18]

He and others argued that while they do not have direct power, participatory power comes from this pressure, with a number of participants indicating that local elected officials sometimes respond because they fear the possibility of popular neighborhood council leaders running against them in municipal elections. The mayor and local civil servants stressed that they are sometimes unable to accept alternatives decided on by citizens due to lack or resources rather than lack of will to do so.

The 6 de Mayo neighborhood council, which has generated medium to high-value outcomes, is a strong example of participants using their mechanisms to achieve outcomes. Local officials demonstrate a strong commitment to the pragmatic citizen participation model and participants were positive about the relationship and their capacity to use this to achieve goals. The relationship is not entirely subordinate, however, and council leaders expressed a willing to use both collaborative and pressure tactics when the need arises. Participants from this council played more of an informal oversight role throughout the process. This, along with the relative openness of the municipal administration to citizen involvement, allowed them to exercise some direct influence. Those responsible for promoting and supporting public participation in 6 de Mayo were generally pleased with the results the commune had achieved and link these outcomes to the relationship between participation and improved governance. Arguing that La Pintana was one of the first Santiago communes to establish an office dedicated to participation, the program director stated that popular participation helps the municipality to better understand and respond to residents' and to work more effectively.

Participants stressed the importance of developing good relationships with both civil servants and elected officials. They pointed out that it is important to maintain these because they cannot simply make demands, as authorities are not obliged to comply regardless of neighborhood council support. The Versalles council's secretary expressed what other members of the directive explained:

> If we go in making demands, they don't have to listen and we could damage the relationship. It works better to write a nice letter requesting a meeting and then go in there with a reasonable proposal that we can say has the support of the community.[19]

The fact that municipal or state officials and technocrats generally take over once projects were decided on did not appear to be a concern for most participants. Furthermore, the councils' leaders explained that they would simply not have the time to dedicate to this as most of their neighbors have jobs and families to care for. They explained that they feel their role is to promote the interests of their neighbors by working with and/or pressuring relevant officials into adopting their councils' decisions, but felt that the implementation work is the responsibility of state officials. They also felt that they are able to use their participatory mechanism to pressure technicians responsible for the projects if they are not carried out according to plan. As Sandra, president of the council put it, if the planning agents and workers are not fulfilling their obligations:

I can go above them, to the head of the department, to the municipal councillors, and these people will listen because they know it is not just me complaining, that I have the entire neighbourhood council behind me, and their support. They will generally put pressure on the technicians to make sure things get done.[20]

The council leaders also stated that the council oversight, even if passive, ensures accountability in that those who are implementing the projects (and managing the funds) "know they are being watched by many eyes." Participants themselves who had benefited from the projects were generally pleased with the projects as implemented by MINVU and their municipal departments. Most in 6 de Mayo and to a lesser extent Versalles claimed that they were directly consulted with respect to how money was to be used for neighborhood improvement projects and that this was a sufficient implementation role as far as they are concerned.

As we have seen, neighborhood councils do not have direct access to their own sources of funding but must request financial support from municipal or central government agencies. This involved either meeting with municipal officials to present requests for specific projects or identifying national programs aimed at specific goals (such as infrastructure) and applying for funds. Councils are required to meet the criteria of the funding agencies and have little control over the money. Venezuelan participants considered access to funds to be an essential factor in terms of ensuring devolution of powers and autonomy. Despite their acceptance of the concept of co-governance, a majority of Chilean respondents interviewed felt that this was a major impediment to neighborhood council autonomy and that governments would have to consider providing more autonomous funding sources if they were serious about enhancing citizen participation.

Deliberation

Chilean neighborhood councils were designed to provide all members with the right to express themselves and to propose initiatives, but there is little mention of the internal deliberation process in the enabling legislation.[21] Unlike in Venezuela, none of the central government officials addressed the quality of deliberation. Most focused on the concepts of co-management and improved governance as discussed in the previous section, but state officials seemed unfamiliar with how neighborhood councils function on a day-to-day basis. A few municipal representatives charged with promoting participation and who have more direct contact with the mechanisms tended to be critical of the internal functioning the councils. While insisting that there is variation in terms of how deliberative these bodies are, they felt that there has not been enough work done to promote internal democracy and deliberation. They attribute the problem to a lack of an institutional framework that encourages and enables the kind of internal democracy that could lead to a better quality of deliberation.

The evidence collected from neighborhood council participants demonstrates mixed results, although the internal process is relatively deliberative for the most part. About half of the participants believed that their neighborhood council provides a deliberative forum characterized by an open, tolerant discussion process; that people are generally listened to when expressing their opinion; and that a variety of options are discussed and weighed. These individuals agree that all council members (as opposed to leaders) are the ones who participate regularly and actively. About half agree that the active members (as opposed to only the leaders) partici-pate in the elaboration of community projects. A majority also believe, however, that some individuals tend to dominate the discussions at least some of the time. There is considerable variation between La Pintana (the higher-value case) and the other two cases.

Among those who were satisfied with the internal workings of their council, most described a process in which people are able to discuss and work with their neighbors in a non-hierarchal setting, something which these respondents appreciate given Chile's rigid social structure. Many of the regular participants described the process in similar terms, arguing that their participation has been a positive experience, that assemblies are always announced ahead of time in order to provide people with reasonable notice, and that most people listen to others and participate respectfully. They attribute "real deliberation" to the absence of hierarchies found in so many other political institutions and groups, often arguing that in dealing with any of the formal institutions, people are made aware of their place in any discussion they have with them, which makes the neighborhood councils a refreshing change. The description of the deliberative process provided by Sandra is similar to that observed in the other cases:

> We call assemblies, the assemblies decide but always after a
> good discussion. We propose, we tell the neighbors what we

suggest but only the assembly can make the decision about what we will bring forward. There can be as much or as little discussion as people want to have, there are no time limits, usually there is friendly disagreement and debate.[22]

But others tended to argue that certain individuals dominate the process because they have been involved for many years and are more familiar with municipal politics. Respondents generally attributed this to the knowledge and expertise that more active and long-term council members had, making these individuals more "authoritative" in council assemblies. The experience gained within participatory mechanisms and in dealing with state institutions is deemed to provide them with an advantage in discussion and debates. Typical of these sentiments is the following comment by Estrella, a participant from Versalles:

They are deliberative in the sense that everyone has the right to participate, to speak and to express opinions, but I'm not sure this is real deliberation because some people—especially the directors and those who have been involved for a long time—know much more than the rest of us about local policies, about how to get things done. We sometimes feel like we don't know what we are talking about, so it is better not to speak and they often seem to assume they know best.[23]

Inclusiveness

The Chilean state discourse surrounding citizen participation bears little resemblance to the other two countries. While the state presents its vision of citizen participation as ensuring that all citizens can participate in decision making, it does not specifically distinguish traditionally excluded sectors (the poor, women, ethnic minorities) as groups that must benefit from participation. Discourse concentrates on the liberal goal of providing all citizens the same political and civil rights. Civil servants charged with coordinating citizen participation focused on developing more effective communication and better relationships between government and citizens through participatory mechanisms.

These cases demonstrate different patterns with respect to this characteristic. The demographic data collected from the surveys for the three Chilean cases reveals that participants are less likely to be drawn from traditionally excluded groups than in Venezuela or Ecuador. With respect to socioeconomic status, only 16% can be identified as precarious/unskilled workers (as compared to 26% in Venezuela) and only 14% as homemakers (compared to 24%). Chilean neighborhood council participants were far more likely than their Venezuelan counterparts to be retired (21%) and professional (16% compared to 3%). Also in contrast to Venezuela, less than half of respondents (47%) earned at or below the monthly minimum wage of 193,000 CLP ($409 US at the time of research).Women are fairly well represented, but make up slightly less than half of participants.

Some residents felt that neighborhood councils were truly inclusive and act as fora for giving a voice to those traditionally excluded from decision making or that these mechanisms provide an expanded role to the poor in decision making. A majority of women believed that women can play an important role in these mechanisms. On a positive note, comparatively few Chileans believed that people are excluded based on political affiliation. Many participants, however, lamented that participation in neighborhood councils tends to be limited. Compared to Venezuela, fewer believed they were inclusive of those with little formal education or that they leverage the experience and abilities of all citizens. One of the most frequently expressed concerns is that neighborhood councils cannot be inclusive because their composition simply is not representative of the communities they are supposed to speak for. All three council presidents acknowledged that younger people rarely participate. Many observed that the same people run the councils year after year and that many of these are older than the general population. These observations about the average age of participants were made by both younger people, who felt the councils were not representative for this reason, and by older people, who lamented the lack of participation from younger neighbors. As Francisco, one of the few students who participates in his neighborhood council, points out:

> But in reality neighborhood councils are not very representative of the neighbours. Most of the people who participate regularly are older people, retired people doing a lot of work but that is not necessarily representative of the interests of the whole community. They are very traditional people who have spent many years doing this and have clientelist relations with the mayor.[24]

Others pointed to the primarily middle-sector representation of most councils' executive organs, arguing that neighborhood councils are not representative of the population because the poorest families in a given neighborhood tend not to participate. As one participant put it: "There are many people who have a level of education that allows them to speak their minds, there are others that have a low level of education and don't want to speak for fear of making a blunder (*meter la pata*)."[25] Local officials, participants, and observers agree that outcomes are likely affected by these patterns; if the local councils are not inclusive, outcomes will not represent the desires and perspectives of a broad range of residents. Regular participants tend to be a small group of people who probably already have influence in a community; and while all local residents can attend assembly meetings and vote, they are not the ones who run things. Directors of municipal departments charged with promoting participation argued that while they had made efforts to engage a greater diversity of participation in neighborhood councils, the fact that council leaders are "always the same" discourages participation.

Levels of Participation

While central government representatives in Chile did not engage with this theme, many of the local officials charged with implementing participatory programs expressed concern over low levels of engagement. They argue that effective participation is hampered by a lack of political education, from childhood through university, which translates into people not knowing how to participate in politics and in community life. Most agree that there is a lack of interest and that if people do organize at all it is not around long-term development but around a very functional short-term project. Furthermore, some local officials and other observers believe that due to Chile's relatively high levels of development, many already feel that their basic needs are satisfied and see little benefit in citizen participation. Similar to the sentiments expressed by local assembly leaders in Ecuador, active participants in Chile felt that this creates an environment in which participation is cyclical, ephemeral, and about "getting something" which is not conducive to building the type of sustained participation that can lead to enhanced governance and an engaged citizenry.

The Chilean cases face some of the same problems as those in Ecuador with respect to levels of participation and ongoing commitment. The

6 de Mayo neighborhood council (the higher-value case) demonstrates a moderate level of participation and engagement. Just over 900 individuals are registered as members and the directive is made up of four individuals. Participation has been high at certain points; as many as 170 individuals have attended assemblies, although this has subsided over the years and attendance now averages about 60 individuals. Still, as many as 100 residents participate when major projects are proposed or significant needs are identified by the community. This level of participation is high by Chilean standards. Council leaders contend, however, that people are more likely to participate in the social events organized by the council. These encourage people to occupy public space and can sometimes be used to discuss political issues with neighbors but, most of the time, people do not show an interest in day-to-day local politics. Only when there is a tangible need are people more likely to re-engage in neighborhood council business. The director of the citizen participation division for La Pintana confirmed that the number of residents who are actively engaged varies, particularly once basic needs are met, and that this diminishes the effectiveness of participation. The participation level tends to correlate with outcomes in this case, however. Minutes and attendance records show that significant outcomes were preceded by high levels of participation. In 2009, the year that the council's largest recent project (housing improvement) was selected, close to 150 individuals attended assemblies in the months prior to the project being adopted. This declined by more than half by the beginning of the following year. Attendance rose again (although not to the same levels) in 2011, when the issue of bringing public transportation into the neighborhood was being discussed and over 90 members participated, but had dropped off again at the time of research (March 2013) to less than 30. Participation in the Versalles case tends to be more limited over time. While the council's registry lists about 600 members, only 30 to 40 individuals participate regularly, although this number can rise to 60 when issues of particular interest to the community arise.

   Some council leaders added to this by touching on a related theme that arose frequently in the Chilean cases. They feel that they do much of the work that the municipality should be doing, but without compensation. These tasks include assessing residents' needs and fixing problems as mundane as advising the relevant municipal department when a street light burns out. Council leaders point out that using these mechanisms for such purposes does not even meet the most basic ideas of citizen participation. The Versalles council's president and finance secretary insisted that they enjoy working for their neighbors but complained that some are extremely "demanding," treating them as though they were municipal employees rather than colleagues in a participatory process. The case also demonstrates some of the generalized concerns discussed above. Council leaders expressed views similar to their counterparts elsewhere, arguing that many residents are more interested in simply receiving benefits than in participatory decision making. The president insisted, for example, that:

> For some, they see this as paid work, but it is not. We are volunteers. Many do not understand that and they come around demanding things. This work takes a lot of time, and we have a house, kids, husbands, over those responsibilities.[26]

Another contrast with the Venezuelan cases involves the extent of participation of ordinary members vs. council leaders. In Venezuela, many communal council members (residents of the neighborhood represented) participated at all stages of the process, from agenda setting to voting to implementation and oversight. In the Versalles case, relatively few members participated beyond the community assembly vote. Council leaders were almost exclusively responsible for moving decisions ahead. Of the individuals interviewed, only two members who were not part of the directive had any role beyond discussing and voting in the assembly. Those who do participate regularly tend to be older, retired residents. Some of these individuals complain that Chileans (particularly of the younger generation) have become increasingly individualistic and that participation in any formal sense is almost anathema.

The Cayumapú case is relatively small as only about 170 individuals are registered as members. Participation has also varied over time but the current president indicated that at recently convened assemblies, only about 20 people attend. Council directive members believe that this is because most people view participation primarily as a means of "getting something." They felt that participation tends to ebb and flow depending on immediate needs, a pattern which they see as contrary to the "spirit of participation" they would like to see.

> When we wanted water, there was a lot of participation, but after getting the network, there was much less. People are not

interested [in] issues unless they want something. When they need things they participate, but when we are successful, that participation ends for many of them. And that is not what participation is about, if we really want to have a say we need to keep up the pressure and that means ongoing and large-scale participation.[27]

The council president also attributes the lack of more recent concrete outcomes to low participation rates, arguing that the lack of involvement diminishes the ability of the council to secure benefits. Active participants identify two reasons for this. If few people participate it is difficult for them to know what their fellow citizens want and what to prioritize. Also, municipal officials know which neighborhood councils have a lot of participation and which ones do not; the heavily supported ones are more likely to achieve outcomes. The council president also insisted that citizen participation can only make a meaningful difference when it is sustained over time and involves the bigger picture, as opposed to people participating because they want some short-term benefit. A number of participants also acknowledged a number of barriers to participation that particularly affect their area, however. Rural districts that are spread out over a large geographical present additional barriers in addition to time constraints, in that some people are required to travel long distances to attend meetings. Those living farther from the central area (generally poorer members of the community) rarely participate because the distance and logistics make this inconvenient.

State-Society Relationships

Like their Ecuadorian counterparts, Chileans involved in these three participatory mechanisms have mixed perceptions of democracy and a moderate sense of political efficacy. A majority of neighborhood council participants felt that democracy works better in their country than in the rest of Latin America, but fewer than in Venezuela felt they had considerable freedom of choice or that they are able to make themselves heard and influence decision making. Citizen participants have a different conception of state-society relationships compared to their counterparts in Venezuela and Ecuador. Chilean neighborhood council participants generally place more importance on the functioning of procedural democracy, on party systems, on individual rights, and on representative institutions. If they do not feel that these are working well (and most do not), there is little sense that participatory mechanisms will enhance democracy. They understand the role of participation as complementary to representative institutions. Yet, as in the other two countries, how citizens conceive of these things aligns with the discourse produced by state institutions, suggesting that in Chile, as in the other two countries, participatory mechanisms act to socialize people into participating in ways that state actors prefer.

Chilean respondents did not qualify democracy by referring to variants. Many respondents were critical about the quality of democracy in their country due to the limited opportunities for citizen participation, but when discussing the concept the common themes that emerged were "free elections," "freedom to do as one pleases," "free speech," and "stability." These conceptions reflect the discursive repertoire found in texts produced by the Chilean state, which links participation to both participatory mechanisms and traditional forms of participation (voting in elections and interacting with elected officials). A more cooperative attitude is expressed with respect to the latter. For example, many respondents said something similar to the following statement offered by an activist in low-income La Pintana (Santiago):

> The primary, and most important act of participation in Chile is voting in national and municipal elections. Participation in the (neighbourhood) council is important yes, but it is equally important that we have elected representatives who care about working with us and helping our communities to develop.[28]

When participation is brought up, it is usually linked to elected representatives and using participation to influence and pressure them (as opposed to direct citizen decision making), as summarized by a participant from Maipú.

> What has come out of this talk about participation is that people are now more likely to have expectations and pressure and make demands of their representatives. This is the most valuable aspect of participation.[29]

In contrast to the other two countries, Chilean respondents rarely used the term "citizen" at all and their conception of "neighbors" (the term used by the state in its participatory discourse) is limited to place (those who live in close proximity) and is not tied discursively to either participation or equality. In the three cases, then, these meanings tend to comply with state discourse on the role of the citizen. The implications of this are significant; "citizen" is a complex concept which entails a series of rights and obligations and suggests belonging to a political community, while "neighbor" refers to individuals who live in close proximity to each other.

State discourse limits the scope of participation to enhancing representative democracy. It contains none of the "revolutionary" discourse found in the other two countries. As with the other two countries, these conceptions are reflected in the discourse of participants. The Chilean state, however, is more likely to recognize participation through channels outside of state mechanisms, such as sports clubs, associations representing seniors, and public interest (education, health and environmental) organizations.

Conclusions

Despite a lack of formal decision-making powers, citizens are able to achieve outcomes by leveraging their relationship with or exerting pressure on officials or through engagement with higher-level institutions that link citizens with local authorities (see summary in table 6.2). They can thus use their participatory mechanisms to get what they want by exercising an indirect role in decision making. Citizens in all of these cases believe that decisions made through the participatory process have more legitimacy than those made by officials alone and they believe that this gives them the right to use participatory mechanisms to pressure elected officials and relevant departments to implement neighborhood council decisions. The quality of internal deliberation, inclusiveness, and levels of participation are important and account for some of the within-country variation, but the most effective outcomes are produced when council participants develop and maintain strong relationships based on mutual trust and respect with local officials.

Table 6.2. Projects, Processes, and Outcomes, Chile

	Alternatives Selected	Process	Outcomes
6 de Mayo	• Homes in need of repair • Improving public lighting • Improving streets and sidewalks • Building sports facilities • Beautification projects (particularly parks) • Access to public transportation	Participants identify needs and select priorities	Medium-High value • Housing improvement projects for over 100 families • Improvement of public lighting over 30 blocks • Improvement of paths and plazas • Sports courts and gym built • Microbus service extended into the community
Versalles	• Homes in need of repair • Improving public lighting • Improving streets and sidewalks • Removal of polluted canal • Crime and security issues	Authorities make final decisions Citizens play a minor role in obtaining funding Implementation carried out by state agencies Subordinate role in relationship with authorities, characterized by cooperation and applying pressure	Medium value • Housing repairs for 48 families, another 43 approved for the program as of 2012 • Repairs and improvements to sidewalks, lighting, etc. • Polluted canal paved over • Liaison program with local police detachment
Cayumapú	• Neighborhood not connected to municipal water supply • Most streets unpaved • Many areas lack public lighting • Housing improvements (roofing)		Medium value • Drinking water extended to homes • Central street paved (100m) • Public lighting in central parts • Housing improvement program

7

Conclusions and Prospects

Venezuelan communal councils, the prototype for the "radical" participatory democracy model in Latin America, produce the highest-value tangible outcomes and the most positive spillover effects. Chilean neighborhood councils, designed according to principles of pragmatic participation and lacking the powers of their Venezuelan counterparts, demonstrate uneven but medium-value outcomes. While the "hard" outcomes are not as significant as in Venezuela, these mechanisms have been relatively successful at achieving tangible benefits for their communities. Ecuador's local citizen assemblies fall short with respect to tangible outcomes, despite the state discourse which appears to place them in the "radical" democracy camp.

The research suggests that quality of deliberation, inclusiveness, levels of participation, and citizen-local government relationships are important characteristics in determining the capacity of participatory mechanisms to produce desirable outcomes. There are notable associations between these factors and the outcomes (see summary in table 7.1). These are strongest in the higher-value outcome cases and practically absent in those that produce less positive outcomes. Decision-making and implementation powers are also important, as the two highest-tier outcome cases are the only ones that fully exercise these powers. The Chilean cases, however, reveal that mechanisms that do not have such formal powers can also produce positive outcomes when citizens and local officials recognize each other's legitimacy in the policy process and are able and willing to work together in productive ways.

Table 7.1. Cases, Characteristics, and Outcomes

Outcomes	Characteristics	Cases
High-Value	High levels of deliberation, inclusiveness and participation; decision-making and implementation powers devolved and fully utilized	Catia, Yagua (Venezuela)
Medium-Value	Moderate levels of deliberation, inclusiveness and participation; decision-making and implementation powers devolved and partially utilized or lack of formal decision-making and implementation powers but informal "observer" role for participants	Belém (Venezuela), 6 de Mayo, Versalles, Cayumapú (Chile), Tarqui (Ecuador)
Low-Value	Low levels of deliberation, inclusiveness and participation; lack of formal decision-making and implementation powers, no informal role sometimes consulted	San Gabriel (Ecuador), Llano Chico (Ecuador)

It does not appear as though the "radical" model of participation is necessarily superior to the "pragmatic" model. While the two highest-value cases are in fact from Venezuela, the poorest outcome cases are Ecuadorian citizens' assemblies which, at least on paper, are designed according to radical participatory principles. State discourse on participatory democracy has even less of an impact on the ability of participatory mechanisms to produce positive tangible outcomes and spillover effects. The Ecuadorian state has engaged in a discourse that promotes a "radical" citizen participation agenda, yet these mechanisms have not produced superior outcomes to their Chilean counterparts, despite the relatively restrained "pragmatic participation" discourse disseminated in that country. Mechanisms that do not demonstrate a high quality of deliberation, inclusiveness, sustained participation, and at least some capacity to engage with local government are not likely to produce desirable outcomes regardless of institutional design and state discourse. When participants and authorities both accept the pragmatic model, strong relationships can be created and participants find ways of using their mechanisms to their advantage by playing an indirect "observer" role in the decision-making process, even when such power has not been formally devolved. When participants expect radical democracy and find that their expectations are not met (Ecuador), these relationships becomes conflictual and positive outcomes are less likely.

This does not mean, however, that institutional design is insignificant. It suggests that policymakers who are serious about promoting citizen participation should pay close attention to these factors rather than to normative, ideologically charged concepts. While focusing on building these factors into the design of participatory mechanisms, policymakers could also learn from the strengths and weaknesses of the radical and pragmatic models.

Strengths and Limitations of Radical and Pragmatic Models of Participatory Design

Both models demonstrate important strengths but also reveal a number of limitations that support the concerns of critics of participatory democracy. Participatory mechanisms can, under the right conditions, allow citizens to achieve significant tangible outcomes that improve their communities. In many of the lower-income neighborhoods studied in this project, residents and local officials agree that these benefits were achieved more effectively due to participation. This supports the idea that participation can produce more equitable access to public goods and services. Many citizens also develop a greater respect for democracy, an enhanced sense of empowerment, and skills that should allow them to participate more effectively with time. There are also limitations that reinforce the concerns expressed in the theoretical literature that is skeptical of participatory democracy. Some of the weaknesses are unique to one model, while others are observable in all cases and speak to broader problems with citizen participation.

The radical Venezuelan model demonstrates significant benefits, particularly with respect to spillover effects, but also has drawbacks. Where they work as expected, communal councils allow citizens to play a significant role in policy that affects their communities and to produce a strong sense of empowerment, and these may have a longer-term societal and political impact than tangible outcomes. Certainly, this model comes closest to the ideals promoted by some of the more "radical" democratic theorists. These results point to a potential for the empowerment of traditionally marginalized sectors. In order to avoid an overly optimistic interpretation of these findings, it is important to highlight that satisfaction with participatory democracy should not be read as uncritical support on the part of participants. Many respondents use the past and/or other countries in the region as reference points. While they may not be entirely pleased with how their participatory mechanisms work in practice, they feel they have more input into decision making than in the past under a relatively closed representative model and believe that they have a greater capacity to participate than in other Latin American countries, which leads to a certain level of satisfaction.

Still, many of the criticisms levelled against radical democracy, and initiatives of the left-leaning governments in particular, emerged in this book. We have seen that they are often politicized and that participation among non-government supporters is low. Whether this is due to intolerance or deliberate self-exclusion (or both), it is clear that there is little room for those who do not share the "radical" Bolivarian ideological agenda and the related conception of democracy. In an institutional context that provides significant formal powers to communal councils at the expense of representative bodies, this raises the sceptre of "tyranny of the (local) majority." Politicization also raises questions about how resources are distributed across participatory mechanisms. This book has studied the various funding sources that participatory mechanisms may draw on to finance their initiatives and argued that this is an important factor when it comes to autonomy. In Venezuela, there are clearly examples of transparent processes at the municipal level that are based on needs assessments and involve citizen representatives. Still, while a fixed a percentage of the national budget is devoted to communal councils, there is little information available with respect to how resources are allotted and divided among the country's various constituencies. This obviously opens the door to regional distribution based on political support, a possibility which is difficult to avoid when funds come from any level of government. While state discourse suggests that resources for participatory mechanisms are distributed according to need, there is little transparency with respect to how funding is actually divided from region to region.

There is an alignment in all three countries between the discourse on citizenship produced by the state and the perceptions of citizen participants. In Venezuela and Ecuador in particular, this includes how participants conceive of democracy and their role in decision making and also extends to the parameters established around citizenship with respect to both acceptable forms of participation and the mechanisms through which this should be exercised. While Venezuelan and Ecuadorian participants conceive of citizen participation as a valued right, the sphere in which they imagine that this can take place is limited. Participation and the exercise of citizenship are linked to a prescribed set of core participatory institutions through which citizens should ideally exercise their rights. In Venezuela, participation is generally equated with communal councils and to a much lesser extent with *comunas* (a new level of government that is supposed to represent multiple communal councils within the same territory) and state-supported social organizations such as urban land committees. In Ecuador, instances of participation are associated with local assemblies and other mechanisms established by the Citizen Participation Law. These patterns can be read as establishing a preferred scope of participation and a distinction between forms that are "legitimate" and those that are framed as either "illegitimate" or ineffective. Ultimately, this may produce results that both expand and contain citizen engagement.

In Chile, state discourse does limit the scope of participation to enhancing representative democracy. It contains none of the "revolutionary" discourse found in the other two countries. As with the other two countries, these conceptions are reflected in the discursive repertoires of participants. The Chilean state, however, is less prescriptive with respect to preferred mechanisms. Participation may be exercised through mechanisms established by state legislation (such as neighborhood councils) but also civil society organizations autonomous from the state, including functional (sports clubs, associations representing seniors, etc.) and public interest organizations. Furthermore, participation is also more likely to be associated with traditional forms of participation (voting in elections, interacting with elected officials) and a more passive and cooperative attitude is expressed with respect to the latter.

Both models demonstrate additional weaknesses which speak to the broader problems with participatory democracy. An important concern involves the scope of influence that participatory mechanisms can have. The communal councils, for example, have been framed as operating in two areas of participatory democracy: addressing local needs through solving community problems in a more inclusive and deliberative manner, and encouraging a broader opening up of political participation. While participatory mechanisms may provide the first, they do not yet allow for engagement with broader political issues beyond local development. While the stated intention of these mechanisms is to provide citizens with both a greater role in everyday decisions that affect their lives and to expand political participation (broadly defined), these experiences have been more successful at achieving the former. The latter goal lags behind, which is not surprising given that it is arguably far more ambitious. It is important to note, however, that these types of institutions are still relatively new and will require time to evolve.

A further problem revolves around the capacity of participants to sustain participation. In many cases, participatory mechanism leaders are taking on a burden that cannot be sustained indefinitely. The implementation and service management components involve the most time-consuming and work-intensive responsibilities, and the burden is often disproportionately shared by those who participate actively. It is unclear how this could be sustained if the mechanisms were to be given greater powers in implementation and management over a broader range of policy areas and services. It is also unclear how long and to what extent the most highly engaged individuals will be willing to take on these responsibilities. There is the danger that what we are witnessing is not the transfer to participatory organizations of powers to implement decisions they make, but rather the downloading of responsibilities and services that the state is incapable of providing. New research could focus on why and under what circumstances citizens decide to participate actively in these mechanisms and on the factors that would encourage more people to do so.

The cases that are deemed to be the least deliberative also suggest that participatory institutions may reproduce domination, racism, and social hierarchies that exist in the types of institutions they are supposed to improve upon. While these problems did not emerge in the more homogenous Venezuelan cases with higher levels of participation, they are a factor in determining why cases with greater disparities between participants fared poorly on the quality of deliberation. In particular, the Ecuadorian cases with significant indigenous populations reveal that racist attitudes prevalent in society are reproduced within the citizens' assemblies. Similarly, there is evidence from at least some of the cases that those with higher levels of education (likely to be more "eloquent") or those more familiar with politics and procedures will have significant advantages in a deliberative process. This will clearly have a negative impact on spillover effects and also presents the danger that tangible outcomes achieved may not reflect the needs of all citizens.

Finally, a number of developments in the region demonstrate the precarious nature of citizen participation initiatives. Participatory mechanisms rely on public funding regardless of whether or not there is a participatory process for distributing the funds. This means that their capacity to function and to implement their decisions is largely based on the economic fortunes of national or local governments. During periods of economic downturn or financial crisis, there will be less money trickling down to fund decisions made at the local level through participatory processes. Participatory governance is vulnerable to the ups and downs of market forces that are entirely beyond the control of citizens or national governments.

Observers across the political spectrum have criticized the Chávez government for retaining the rentier, petro-state model, which has intensified the Venezuelan economy's dependence on oil. Oil rents made it possible to import goods required to meet people's basic needs and to pay for the government's extensive social investments. They also served to fund the various agencies that provide resources to communal councils. The collapse of oil prices, beginning in 2014, reduced the price per barrel from $100 US in 2013 to $24.25 US in February 2016 and pushed the Venezuelan economy into a deep recession that Chávez's successor Nicolás Maduro has been unable to address. According to the Economic Commission for Latin America and the Caribbean (ECLAC), Venezuela's GDP shrank by 3.9% in 2014 and 5.7% in 2015, and its inflation rate surpassed 180.9% by 2015. Not surprisingly, this has a significant impact on the resources that are available to participatory mechanisms.

In 2017 Venezuela's economic troubles were further compounded by the country's most serious political crisis since the failed coup of 2002. President Maduro's efforts to establish a constituent assembly to rewrite the constitution provoked condemnation from opposition forces and international observers and led to violent clashes between protestors and state forces in Caracas. Critics charged that Maduro sought to dismantle democratic institutions at the national level in order to concentrate power in the hands of the Executive. The outcome of these developments is unclear as this book goes to press, as are the implications for local participatory democracy.

The Ecuadorian economy, which had been characterized by unprecedented growth and strong social investment during much of Correa's administration, also began to falter from 2015 onward. While not as dependent on oil as Venezuela, Ecuador's oil revenue fell by 50% from 2014 to 2015. This has diminished the government's ability to sustain social spending, including allotting funds for participatory mechanisms. The country's economy was further damaged by a powerful earthquake in April 2016, which caused extensive damage to the coastal areas (including the city of Manta where the Tarqui neighborhood was largely destroyed). The government estimated reconstruction costs at nearly 3 percentage points of GDP.

These developments endanger the social achievements of the previous decade, including the power of participatory mechanisms which rely on public funding to implement the various development projects they decide on. While the research presented in this book was conducted before the economic decline that began in 2014, follow-up conversations with communal council and local assembly spokespeople suggests that participatory mechanisms have suffered in terms of access to funding. This does not necessarily mean that participatory mechanisms are doomed, however. Venezuela's main opposition leaders have pledged to maintain the country's system of communal councils, although they claim that these mechanisms must be de-politicized. In fact, research suggests that municipalities controlled by center-right parties can and do support successful participatory initiatives, as participatory democracy has become deeply entrenched across the Venezuelan political spectrum (Hetland 2014). Given the benefits that they provide to marginalized communities and the commitment of a large segment of the population to citizen participation, participatory mechanisms should be able to weather the storm. However, it is likely that they will continue to be subject to economic cycles like any other state-funded program, which has implications for the long-term role of citizens in decision making.

Improving Participatory Mechanisms: A Focus on the Key Factors of Success

Those committed to enhancing the capacity of participatory institutions to produce positive outcomes must focus on the quality of deliberation, inclusiveness, the level of engagement, and commitment and relationships between citizen participants and relevant government agencies.

The quality of deliberation is complex, but looking at the more and less successful cases suggests a number of problems that need to be addressed by those who design and promote participation. High and lower outcome cases were distinguished by the extent to which participants felt they could express themselves openly and expect others to listen to them. The lower-tier outcome cases were characterized by a narrower range of topics open for discussion, group rivalries, and a sense that some members dominate the discussion. In some cases, certain individuals are reluctant to participate because they felt they are less articulate or well-informed than the more vocal members of the community.

While these problems are difficult to resolve in any social setting, the importance of ensuring a deliberative environment requires attention from officials who wish to develop stronger participatory mechanisms. First, it is essential to ensure that all citizen participants have access to the information they require to engage in meaningful deliberation with their peers. In most cases observed in this research, the leaders of participatory mechanisms provide information. This allows certain individuals significant control and advantages. State agencies can assist participatory mechanisms in establishing a system of effective and equal information dissemination. Such a system could involve procedures to ensure that all participants have access to the same information before any deliberation is allowed to commence.

Second, state agencies must establish clear (and systematically enforced) procedures surrounding the deliberative process itself to ensure that participants speak and listen in a respectful manner. This would also include a methodology for weighing different perspectives and making decisions when consensus is not possible. All participants must be allotted equal time and some type of sanction for those who do not play by the rules may be required.

Venezuelan and Ecuadorian state agencies have made some efforts to provide these guidelines. Both have developed workshops to "teach" citizens how to deliberate with others, and agencies have distributed training manuals that attempt to establish rules and procedures for effective participatory deliberation. However, there are no mechanisms to ensure that these guidelines are implemented within local institutions, and training is generally provided only when a participatory mechanism is launched. The ability for participants to file a grievance if they find that their local assembly is not producing a deliberative environment could help ensure that procedures are followed. Having a "participation specialist" from a state agency attend meetings of newly established local assemblies could help to provide feedback to participants and leaders. Of course, to ensure legitimacy this involvement would need to be restricted to supporting the quality of deliberation and not be seen as intervening in the content of discussions. Training opportunities should be ongoing, although such efforts must not overburden participants who have busy lives. Additional training for those who feel they require it, including public speaking for individuals who are intimidated about expressing themselves in a public forum, could be beneficial. Finally, alternative means of engaging in deliberation, including the use of online tools, could expand opportunities to participate—providing that adequate training and access to technology are provided to all members.

Inclusiveness is clearly a key factor in the success of participatory institutions, but is difficult to ensure in practice due to a number of barriers identified in this research. Participatory mechanisms in the three countries have been successful at attracting large numbers of people from groups that have been traditionally excluded from the policymaking process, particularly women and the poor. The fact that these groups are members of these institutions is only one part of the story, however. In the cases that produced the most disappointing tangible outcomes and spillover effects, we find that power relations that exist in society and traditional institutions are reproduced within the mechanisms themselves. This includes instances of paternalistic behavior and racism. Clearly, the quality of deliberation and inclusiveness are closely interrelated; the cases that are deemed to be less deliberative also fare poorly with respect to inclusiveness. Comparing the cases also suggests some possible paths for improvement, however. Some of the solutions discussed under deliberation would also help to address some of these problems: an equitable system of information dissemination, clear and well-enforced procedures for ensuring that all members are treated equally, and training and mechanisms that individuals can call on when their peers do not play by the rules. Participatory mechanisms and the agencies that support them must also make targeted efforts to attract members of racialized minorities and to ensure that their specific grievances are recognized. This can include initiatives such as Black History programs and promoting Indigenous cultural events depending on the membership.

Studying inclusiveness also revealed additional concerns not directly related to power relations. These include an apparent lack of interest among certain segments of society (particularly youth) and barriers based on lack of time and distance from meeting venues. While it would be impossible to entirely resolve such problems, states that are genuinely committed to ensuring inclusiveness can consider various measures. Guidelines can ensure that meeting times and locations rotate to accommodate different work schedules and geographic proximity. Labor legislation can support citizens who wish to exercise their right to participate just as employers are required to offer staff time off for activities such as voting and jury duty. At the time of this research, the Venezuelan government was considering reform that would reduce the work week for those actively engaged in participatory mechanisms. Opportunities for involvement in the various functions and activities of the participatory mechanisms can be expanded through information and communications technologies. Providing online fora for participatory engagement may also help to attract younger citizens, who demonstrate low rates of participation across the three countries. This would, of course, necessitate state participation agencies offering appropriate training and access to technology to citizens who require such support, particularly in poor and indigenous communities. Such training would benefit the recipients beyond participatory mechanisms, and states should see this as contributing to the social development of marginalized communities.

Achieving and sustaining high levels of participation is another important factor. Lack of participation may sometimes be related to the issues discussed above (lack of time, geographic distance from meeting places, etc.). For these citizens, the solutions discussed above may help to address the barriers they face. Of course, other explanations for low levels of participation are beyond the control of those who design participatory mechanisms. Many citizens will remain apathetic and uninterested in public participation regardless of accessibility of opportunities for engagement. The "free rider" problem is well known in the collective action literature and extends to citizen participation. These individuals may calculate that they are able to receive a benefit or public good even if they do not participate in their local communal council or citizens' assembly. Experts charged with promoting participatory initiatives must closely study what incites people to engage. We have seen, for example, that neighbors are more likely to participate when they perceive that something significant is being discussed and when they believe that significant results will be achieved.

This suggests a need for better communication between participatory mechanisms and residents who do not participate regularly. Leaders must ensure that they solicit feedback from the entire community and not only from regular participants. This can help to ensure that nonparticipants' needs are taken into account and that they see their wishes reflected in what is being discussed. State agencies can assist council and assembly leaders to coordinate this communication and disseminate information. The latter activity must also focus on making residents aware of the achievements of their participatory mechanism.

With respect to ensuring efficient and productive working relationships between citizen participants and local authorities, a key problem observed in this study is related to the alignment between expectations and reality. It is important that citizens, government agencies, central state and local politicians, and civil servants be on the same page. State discourse should not promise a level of democracy that institutions cannot or will not provide in practice. Lack of alignment on this factor produces tensions that make progress difficult. Design of participatory systems must also avoid overlapping powers or ambiguous divisions of power between citizens and officials. Formal devolution of decision-making and implementation powers can empower citizens, but the most important consideration is that citizens can engage in these processes in meaningful ways. If formal powers are not fully devolved, there must be organs in place to ensure that relationships can be effective, non-conflictual and (ideally) institutionalized. The Chilean cases that produced positive outcomes despite a lack of formal decision-making and implementation powers were all able to engage with local or state officials through some kind of municipal or regional-level mechanism. In most cases, authorities played a dominant role within these organs but there is no reason why they cannot be redesigned to provide a more equal balance of power. Central state agencies committed to citizen participation can design and enforce the development of regional participatory organs that are more institutionalized than the current iterations. They should have clear procedures that allow for respectful interaction between citizen representatives and authorities.

Final Reflections

It is clear from interviews with politicians and civil servants in these three countries that despite cynical musings about the true intentions of these initiatives, many of these individuals are genuinely committed to enhancing the quality of democracy at the local level. The research presented in this book should contribute to informing those charged with expanding participation. Both the radical and pragmatic models demonstrate strengths and limitations. Ideally, future participatory innovations could draw on elements of both to produce stronger participatory mechanisms and limit the shortcomings of each model. This would involve providing citizens with a real role in decision making while maintaining the checks and balances of representative institutions. Future research could consider what such a model would look like.

Ultimately, efforts should focus on the factors that produce positive outcomes. States have engaged in a battle of ideas over the nature of democracy, the role of citizen participation, and the ideal balance between citizens and authorities in the process. The importance of the factors discussed in this book suggests that they should be focusing on practical areas of institutional design by more effectively operationalizing deliberation, inclusiveness, productive citizen-government relationships and promoting high levels of participation. Ensuring that the design of participatory mechanisms incorporates these characteristics to the extent possible should be given precedence over developing models based on elusive concepts and ideologically charged discourse.

Despite the limitations of the different participatory models developed in Venezuela, Ecuador and Chile, all three countries have promoted a more active and inclusive citizenship than in the past. The value of citizen participation has been acknowledged across the political spectrum and opposition forces in all three countries have pledged to maintain the participatory mechanisms established by left-leaning governments, although they claim to be committed to their de-politicization.

Both participatory and liberal democrats must remain vigilant in order to ensure that mechanisms designed to deepen democracy are not used to impose controlled inclusion. This is particularly important in the context of still-fragile Latin American democracies characterized by strong Executives and weak checks and balances at the national level. At the same time, we must avoid the elitist critiques that implicitly or explicitly frame marginalized actors as irrational and easily manipulated. This perspective tends to characterize much of the media coverage and follows a tradition in one current of the academic literature that perceives the lower strata as prone to irrational impulses and incapable of critical analysis in their assessment of politics.

A segment of the historically marginalized sectors of the population has now experienced some form of inclusion in decision making and perceives this as a fundamental right. Even where instrumental outcomes are less significant and participants are not satisfied with the actual participatory processes, people value the "on paper" right to participate as a good in itself. These effects may very well outlast the political movements that initiated the participatory discourse.

Notes

Chapter 3

1. Universidad Bolivariana de Venezuela, *Formación consejos comunales.*
2. MPComunas, *Guía de formulación de proyectos.*
3. Interviews with G. Valero, Project Support Agent, CORPOANDES, Mérida, Nov. 21, 2012; Nelly Gutiérrez, Director of Communal Development, Consejo federal de gobierno, Mérida, Nov. 15, 2012; Francois Albarrán, Coordinador, Taquilla Unica, Fundacomunal, Mérida, Nov. 13, 2012.
4. Consejo federal de gobierno, *Plan de inversión comunal and Modelo de autoconstrucción*; Francois Albarrán, Coordinador, Taquilla Unica, Fundacomunal Mérida, Nov. 13, 2012.
5. Ecuador, *Ley Orgánica de Participación Ciudadana (2010)*; CPCCS, *Políticas de participación ciudadana.*
6. SENPLADES, *Guía de participación ciudadana.*
7. Interview with Pamela Troya, Participation Advisor, CPCCS, Quito, Oct. 12, 2012; CPCCS, *Las Asambleas Locales Ciudadanas.*
8. Interview with Ana Maria Larrea, Deputy Minister, SENPLADES, Quito, Oct. 25, 2012.
9. Interviews with Emilifran Pazmiño and Marlene Jarrin, Participation Advisors, CPCCS, Quito, Oct. 28, 2012; Viviana García, Participation Advisor, CPCSS, Guayaquil, Feb. 21, 2013.
10. CPCCS, *Curso de Participación Ciudadana, Control Social y Rendición de Cuentas.*
11. *Biblioteca Nacional de Chile*, Guía legal sobre juntas de vecinos.
12. Interviews with Thomás Marín, Director of Citizen Participation, Municipalidad de Providencia, March 14, 2013; Monica Jarra, Head of Community Organizations division, Municipalidad de La Pintana, March 19, 2013; Sandra and Maria Teresa, council president and secretary, Maipú, March 14, 2013; Gloria, council president, La Pintana, March 22, 2013.
13. Chile, *Ley sobre asociaciones y participación ciudadana en la gestión pública (2011)*; MSGG, División de Organizaciones Sociales, *La Participación Ciudadana como Eje de Gestión del Gobierno.*

Chapter 4

1. Instituto Nacional de Estadística, Censos de Población y Vivienda (http://www.ine.gob.ve).

2. One of the so-called Bolivarian Missions, Gran Misión Vivienda is intended to provide housing for those who cannot afford it.

3. Consejo Comunal Sector EC, *Propuesta Proyecto de Colacas*, 2006; *Propuesta Mejoramiento de Vivienda, 2008.*

4. Interview with Nere, Caracas, Jan. 16, 2013.

5. Funadcomunal Caracas, *Informe "Memoria y Cuenta" 2008*; Consejo Comunal Sector EC and SINATECC, *Plan comunitario de desarrollo integral: Sistema de Cloacas.*

6. Fondo Intergubernamental para la Descentralización, another central state fund that finances communal council projects.

7. Consejo Comunal Sector EC and Sistema Nacional de Apoyo Técnico a los Consejos Comunales (SINATECC), *Plan comunitario de desarrollo integral: Sistema de Cloacas.*

8. Interviews with Coordinator of Communal Technical Support, Jan. 21, 2013, and Technical Support Agent for Communal Councils, Fundacomunal Caracas, 23, 2013.

9. Interview with Javi, council participant, Caracas, Jan. 13, 2013.

10. Consejo Comunal Sector EC and SINATECC, *Plan comunitario de desarrollo integral 2009–2010.*

11. Interview with Martin, council participant, Caracas, Jan. 11, 2013.

12. Consejo Comunal Sector EC and SINATECC, *Plan comunitario de desarrollo integral 2011–2012.*

13. Interview with Iris, council participant, Caracas, Jan. 25, 2013.

14. CC Sector EC, *Acta de la reunión de la Asamblea Ciudadana*, May 12, 2012.

15. CC Los Cabos, Actas de la reunión de la asamblea ciudadana, 21 Oct. 2009; and interviews with members of communal council executive, Guacara, Nov. 26 and 27, 2012.

16. CC Los Cabos and Instituto Municipal de Formación Técnico Comunitaria (Guacara), *Plan de desarrollo comunitario, 2012–2013* and interviews with Helen, Raquel, Maria, and Maricruz, Nov. 26 and 27, 2012.

17. CC Los Cabos and Instituto Municipal de Formación Técnico Comunitaria (Guacara), *Plan de desarrollo comunitario, 2012–2013.*

18. Interview with Geraldina, communal council participant, Nov. 29, 2012.

19. Interview with Anita, communal council participant, Guacara, Nov. 29, 2012.

20. CC Los Cabos and Instituto Municipal de Formación Técnico Comunitaria (Guacara), *Plan de desarrollo comunitario, 2012–2013.*

21. Interview with Maria S., Guacara, Nov. 26, 2012.

22. Interview with Maricruz, communal council secretary, Guacara, Nov. 26, 2012.

23. Consejo Comunal Subsector 21 Belén, *Actas de la asamblea*, Nov. 2009.

24. Corpoandes Mérida, *Memoría y Cuenta 2011*.

25. Interview with Yolanda, Merida, Nov. 16, 2012.

26. Interview with Maryenella, Mérida, Nov. 9, 2012

27. Interview with Carla, Mérida, Nov. 17, 2012.

28. Hugo Chávez, Alo Presidente, #244, Jan. 15, 2006.

29. Interview with Alirio Ríos, Director for Communal Management, Fundacomunal, Caracas, Jan. 21, 2013.

30. Interview with Sectional Executive Committee head, Acción Democrática (AD), Mérida, Nov. 11, 2012.

31. Interview with Max, Guacara, Nov. 28, 2012.

32. Interview with Marbella, Mérida, Nov. 14, 2012.

33. Interview with José Luis, Guacara, Dec. 3, 2012

34. Interview with Geora Valero, Mérida, Nov. 21, 2012.

35. Interview with Blanca, Caracas, Jan. 8, 2013.

36. Interview with Marisol, Caracas, Jan. 16, 2013.

37. Interview with Henrick, council participant, Caracas, Jan. 10, 2013.

38. Interview with Nelly Gutiérrez, Corporación de los Andes, Mérida, Nov. 21, 2012.

39. Interview with Fer, Caracas, Jan. 7, 2013.

40. Interviews with two officials, one from the Parish of Arias (Mérida) and one from the Municipality of Mérida, Nov. 9, 2012.

41. Interview with Reinaldo, council president, Mérida, Nov. 15, 2012.

42. Interview with Alirio Ríos, Caracas, Jan. 21, 2013.

43. Interview Iris, Caracas, Jan. 25, 2013.

44. Interview with Helen, Guacara, Nov. 26, 2012.

45. Interview with Alina, Caracas, Jan. 11, 2013.

46. Interview with Ignacio, Caracas, Jan. 19, 2013.

47. Interview with Francisco, Caracas, Jan. 8, 2013.

48. Interview with Marbella, Mérida, Nov. 14, 2012.

49. Interview with Chela, Mérida, Nov. 8, 2012.

50. Hugo Chávez, Alo Presidente, #244, Jan. 15, 2006.

51. Interview with Senior Official, National Strategy for Communes, MPComunas, Caracas, Jan. 25, 2013.

52. This was the official minimum wage at the time this research was conducted. It amounts to about $472 US at the official government exchange rate (which is inaccessible to most Venezuelans) but much less as the market rate.

53. Interview with Raquel, Guacara, Nov. 26, 2012.

54. Interview with Fer, council participant, Caracas, Jan. 7, 2013.

55. Interview with Juan Carlos, council participant, Guacara, Dec. 8, 2012.

56. Interview with Geraldina, communal council participant, Nov. 29, 2012.

57. Interview with Fer, council participant, Caracas, Jan. 7, 2013.

58. Interview with Laura, council participant, Caracas, Jan. 22, 2013.

59. Interview with Geraldina, Guacara, Nov. 29, 2012.

60. Interview with Raquel, council executive member, Guacara, Nov. 26, 2012.

61. Interview with Angel, Mérida, Nov. 10, 2012.

62. Interview with Leandro, Caracas, Jan. 10, 2013.

63. Interview with Francisco, Caracas, Jan. 8, 2013.

64. Interview with G. Valero, Project Support Agent, Corpoandes, Mérida, Nov. 21, 2012.

65. Of Venezuelan participants, a strong majority (81%, n = 152) identified themselves as supporters of the ruling Partido Socialista Unido de Venezuela (PSUV) founded by former president Hugo Chávez (1999–2013).

66. Interview with Erik Uzcategui, Leader of the Movimiento 13 de Marzo, Mérida, Nov. 8, 2012.

67. Interview with Yelitza, communal council participant, Guacara, Nov. 27, 2012.

68. Interview with Miriana, Caracas, Jan. 22, 2013.

69. Interview with Anita, Guacara, Nov. 29, 2012.

70. Interview with Chela, Merida, Nov. 8, 2012.

71. Interview with Francisco, Caracas, Jan. 8, 2013.

72. Texts produced by *Servicio Autónomo Fondo Nacional de los Consejos Comunales* (SAFONACC), *Escuela Fortalecimiento del Poder Popular, Fondo Intergubernamental para la Descentralización (FIDES), Fundación escuela de gerencia social, Universidad Bolivariana de Venezuela.*

73. Interview with Carla, Mérida, Nov. 17, 2012.

74. Interview with Francisco, Caracas, Jan. 8, 2013.

Chapter 5

1. Instituto de la Ciudad, *Censo de Población y Vivienda y del Censo Económico 2010.*

2. *Censo de Población y Vivienda 2010.*

3. Asamblea de participación ciudadana y control social de la Parroquia Tarqui, *Informe 2012–2013* and interviews with assembly executive members, Manta, Feb. 4, 2013.

4. GAD de Manta, *Plan de Obra Anual 2013.*

5. GAD de Manta, *Plan de Obra Anual 2013.*

6. Interview with Councillor, Municipio de Manta, Feb. 6, 2013.

7. Interview with Jose B, Manta, Feb. 4, 2013.

8. Interview with Franklin, Manta, Feb. 4, 2013.

9. GAD de Manta, Boletín informativo del Gobierno Autónomo Descentralizado del Cantón Manta (GAD-Manta); Manta, *Ordenanza que crea y regula el sistema de participación de Manta* (2011).

10. Interviews with assembly participants José, Feb. 4, 2013; Ketty, Manta, Feb. 9, 2013; Betty, Manta, Feb. 11, 2013; and see Manta, *Ordenanza que crea y regula el sistema de participación de Manta* (2011).

11. Asamblea de Unidad Cantonal de Montúfar, *Informe Coordinación general AUCM,* Jan. 2010; interviews with assembly executive members, San Gabriel, Oct. 14, 2012.

12. Interview with Blanca, San Gabriel, Oct. 21, 2012.

13. Interview with Efran, San Gabriel, Oct. 14, 2012.

14. Actas de la reunión de la asamblea ciudadana, mayo 2011.

15. Interview with Maria, assembly participant, Quito, Sept. 23, 2012.

16. Interview with Isabel Terán, Deputy Minister, Secretaría General de la Gobernación La Secretaría General de la Gobernación, Quito, Oct. 11, 2012.

17. Interview with Ana Maria Larrea, Deputy Minister, SENPLADES, Quito, Oct. 25, 2012.

18. Interview with Councillor, Municipio de Manta, Feb. 6, 2013.

19. Interview with assembly executive member, Montúfar, Oct. 14, 2012.

20. Interview with José, Manta, Feb. 4, 2013.

21. Interview with Efran, council participant, Montúfar, Oct. 14, 2012.

22. Interview with Betty, Manta, Feb. 11, 2013.

23. Interview with Salomé, council participant, Calderón, Oct. 3, 2012.

24. Ecuador, *Ley Orgánica de Participación Ciudadana*; Consejo de participación ciudadana y control social (CPCCS), http://www.participacionycontrolsocial. gov.ec/; *Conceptos básicos de la participación, Las Asambleas Locales Ciudadanas y el Sistema de participación ciudadana en las localidades*; Secretaría Nacional de Planificación y Desarrollo (SENPLADES), *Guía de participación ciudadana en la planificación de los GADs, La participación ciudadana para la vida democrática.*

25. Interview with Isabel Terán, Deputy Minister, Secretaría General de la Gobernación La Secretaría General de la Gobernación, Quito, Oct. 11, 2012.

26. Interview with Byron Obando, Director of Citizen Initiatives, Secretaría de Pueblos, Quito, Oct. 9, 2012.

27. Interview with Betty, assembly secretary, Manta, Feb. 11, 2013.

28. Interview with Miriam council participant, Calderón, Oct. 3, 2012.

29. Interview with Patty, San Gabriel, Oct. 17, 2012.

30. Based on attendance records and estimations provided by participatory mechanism leaders.

31. Interview with Franklin, citizens' assembly executive member, Manta, Feb. 4, 2013.

32. Interview with Blanca O, assembly participant, Manta, Oct. 21, 2012.

33. Interview with Christian, citizens' assembly participant, Ibarra, Oct. 30, 2012.

34. Interview with José, citizens' assembly executive member, Manta, Feb. 4, 2013.

35. Interview with Miriam, citizens' assembly participants, Carcelén, Oct. 3, 2012.

36. Interview with Blanca O, assembly participant, Manta, Oct. 21, 2012.

37. Interview with Franklin, citizens' assembly executive member, Manta, Feb. 4, 2013.

38. Interview with Rosita F, participant, Calderón, Oct. 3, 2012.

Chapter 6

1. Ministerio de Desarrollo Social, *Encuesta de Caracterización Socioeconómica Nacional (CASEN)*, 2011; INE, *Clasificación Socioeconómica de Hogares de Chile*.

2. La Pintana, *Revista 6 de Mayo Edición Aniversario*.

3. Junta de Vecinos 6 de Mayo, *Informe anual 2010*.

4. MINVU, *Subsidios para Reparación y Mejoramiento de la Vivienda*. Retrieved from www.minvu.cl.

5. La Pintana, *Revista 6 de Mayo*.

6. MINVU, *Programa Quiero mi Barrio*. Retrieved from www.minvu.cl.

7. Junta de Vecinos Versalles 2, *Registro*.

8. Junta de Vecinos Camino Real, Informe 2012.

9. Interview with Carla Parraguez, Citizen Participation Advisor, Ministerio Secretaría General de Gobierno, La Moneda, Santiago, Mar. 19, 2013.

10. Interview with Francisco Estévez, Former Director of the Social Organizations Division, Ministry of the Government, Santiago, Mar. 18, 2013.

11. Interview with J. Alarcon, Ministry of Justice, Santiago, Mar. 22, 2013.

12. Interview with Municipal Councillor, Maipú, Apr. 5, 2013.

13. Interviews with Gonzalo Delamaza, Professor, Universidad de Los Lagos, Santiago, Mar. 14, 2013; Juan Salinas, Coordinator, Association of Chilean Municipalities, Mar. 18, 2013.

14. Interview with the Pablo G., Valdivia, Chile, Mar. 28, 2013.

15. Interview with Gloria R., La Pintana, Chile, Mar. 22, 2013.

16. Interview with Pablo, council president, Valdivia, Apr. 20, 2013.

17. Interview with Gloria, council president, La Pintana, Mar. 22, 2013.

18. Interview with Pablo G., Valdivia, Apr. 20, 2013.

19. Interview with Maria Teresa, Maipú, Mar. 14, 2013.

20. Interview with Sandra, council president, Maipú, Mar. 14, 2013.

21. Biblioteca nacional de Chile, *Guía legal sobre Juntas de vecinos*; Chile, *Ley sobre asociaciones y participación ciudadana en la gestión pública*; Gobierno de Chile, *Participación Ciudadana*, http://www.participacionciudadana.gob.cl; Ministerio Secretaría general de gobierno, División de Organizaciones Sociales, *La Participación Ciudadana como Eje de Gestión del Gobierno, Política para la participación ciudadana en el marco de la corresponsibilidad*.

22. Interview with Sandra, council president, Maipú, Mar. 14, 2013.

23. Interview with Estrella, council participant, Maipú, Mar. 17, 2013.

24. Interview with Francisco, council participant, Maipú, Mar. 18, 2013.

25. Interview with Renan, council member, Cayumapú, Apr. 21, 2013.

26. Interview with Sandra, council president, Maipú. Mar. 14, 2013.

27. Interview with Ariel, council participant, Cayumapú, Apr. 21, 2013.

28. Interview with Luis A., neighborhood council vice-president, La Pintana, Mar. 23, 2013.

29. Interview with Maria Teresa, neighborhood council secretary, Maipú, Mar. 14, 2013.

Works Cited

Abelson, J., & Gauvin, F-P. (2006). *Assessing the Impacts of Public Participation: Concepts, Evidence and Policy Implications.* Ottawa: Canadian Policy Research Networks.

Abers, R. (2000). *Inventing Local Democracy: Grassroots Politics in Brazil.* Boulder, CO; London: Lynne Rienner.

Aguilera, C. (2007). Participación ciudadana en el gobierno de Bachelet: Consejos asesores presidenciales. *América Latina Hoy, 46,* 143–99.

Altschuler, D., & Corrales, J. (2012). The Spillover Effects of Participatory Governance: Evidence from Community-Managed Schools in Honduras and Guatemala. *Comparative Political Studies*, 45(5), 636–66.

Armony, A. (2004). *Dubious Link: Civic Engagement and Democratization.* Stanford, CA: Stanford University Press.

Arnstein, S. (1969). A Ladder of Citizen Participation. *Journal of the American Institute of Planners*, 35(4), 216–24.

Avritzer, L. (2009). *Participatory Institutions in Democratic Brazil.* Washington, DC; Baltimore: Woodrow Wilson Center Press: Johns Hopkins University Press.

———. (2002). *Democracy and the public space in Latin America.* Princeton, NJ: Princeton University Press.

Baiocci, G. (2003). The Porto Alegre Experiment. In *Deepening Democracy: Institutional Innovations in Empowered Participatory Governance.* London; New York: Verso.

Baiocchi, G., Heller, P., & Silva, M. (2011). *Bootstrapping Democracy: Transforming Local Governance and Civil Society in Brazil.* Stanford, CA: Stanford University Press.

Barber, B. (1984). *Strong Democracy: Participatory Politics for a New Age.* Berkeley: University of California Press.

Barrett, G, Wyman, M., & Coehlo. V. (2012). Assessing the Policy Impacts of Deliberative Citizen Engagement. In Nabatchi, Tina et al. *Democracy in Motion: Evaluating the Practice and Impact of Deliberative Civic Engagement.* New York: Oxford University Press.

Bates, C. (2003). *Aristotle's "Best Regime": Kingship, Democracy, and the Rule of Law*. Baton Rouge: Louisiana State University Press.

Beetham, D. (1999). *Democracy and Human Rights*. Cambridge, UK: Polity Press.

Berelson, B. (1954). *Voting; A Study of Opinion Formation in a Presidential Campaign*. Chicago: University of Chicago Press.

Bourdieu, P. (1991). *Language and Symbolic Power*. Cambridge, MA: Harvard University Press.

Burbach, R., & Piñeiro, C. (2007). Venezuela's Participatory Socialism. *Socialism and Democracy 21*(3), 181–200.

Burron, N. (2012). Unpacking U.S Democracy Promotion in Bolivia: From Soft Tactics to Regime Change. *Latin American Perspectives 38*(1), 96–114.

Burton, P. (2009). Measuring the Benefits of Public Participation. *Evaluation. 15*(3), 263–84.

Cameron, M., Hershberg, E., & Sharpe, K. (2012). New Institutions for Participatory Democracy in Latin America. New York: Palgrave McMillian.

Castañeda, J. (2006). Latin America's Left Turn. *Foreign Affairs*, May/June.

Castañeda, J., & Morales, M. (2008). *Leftovers: Tales of the Latin American Left*. New York: Routledge.

Checa, L.; Lira, L., & Cabalin, C. (2011). El caso de Chile durante el gobierno de Michelle Bachelet. Participación ciudadana para el fortalecimiento de la democracia. *Argos, 28*(55), 13–47.

Chile, Republica de. (2011). *Ley sobre asociaciones y participación ciudadana en la gestión pública*.

———. (2011b). *Guía legal sobre juntas de vecinos*.

———. (1997). *Ley sobre juntos de vecinos y demás organizaciones comunitarias*.

Cleuren, H. (2007). Local Democracy and Participation in Post-Authoritarian Chile. *European Review of Latin American and Caribbean Studies*, 83, 3–18.

Cohen, J. (1997). Procedure and Substance in Deliberative Democracy, in *Deliberative Democracy: Essays on Reason and Politics*. Cambridge, MA: MIT Press.

Cohen, J. and Arato, A. (1992). *Civil Society and Political Theory*. Cambridge, MA: MIT Press.

Cohen, J., & Fung, A. (2004). Radical Democracy. *Swiss Journal of Political Science, 10*(4).

Cohen, J., Rogers, J., Wright, Olin E., & Hirst, P. (1995). *Associations and Democracy*. London; New York: Verso.

Colburn, F., & Trejos, A. (2010). Democracy Undermined: Constitutional Subterfuge in Latin America. *Dissent 57*(3), 11–15.

Corrales, J. (2006). The Many Lefts of Latin America. *Foreign Policy*, December 2006.

Crespo, S. (2008). Citizen Participation: The Constitution of 1998 and the New Constitutional Project. *Iconos: Revista De Ciencias Sociales*, 32, 13–7.

Cunill Grau, N. (1997). *Repensando lo público a través de la sociedad. Nuevas formas de gestión pública y representación social*. Venezuela: CLAD y Nueva Sociedad.

————. (2008). "La construcción de ciudadanía desde una institucionalidad pública ampliada," en Mariani, R. (Coord.), Contribuciones al debate: Democracia/ Estado/Ciudadanía Hacia un Estado de y para la democracia en América Latina. Vol. II. PNUD-UE, 113–38.

Delli Carpini, M., Cook, F., & Jacobs, L. (2004). Public Deliberation, Discursive Participation and Citizen Engagement: A Review of the Empirical Literature, *Annual Review of Political Science*, 7, 315–44.

de la Torre, C., & Peruzzotti, E. (2008). El regreso del populismo. In eds. Carlos de la Torre and Felipe Burbano, *El retorno del pueblo: Populismo y nuevas democracias en América Latina*, Quito: FLACSO, 125–60.

Domínguez, J. (2003). Constructing Democratic Governance in Latin America. In Domínguez and Shifter. *Constructing Democratic Governance in Latin America*. Baltimore, MD: Johns Hopkins University Press.

Ecuador, Republica del. (2010). *Participación Ciudadana*. http://www.participacionycontrolsocial.gov.ec/web/guest/promocion

————. (2010b). *Ley Orgánica de Participación Ciudadana*.

————. (2008). *Nueva Constitución Política del Estado*. http://pdba.georgetown. edu/Constitutions/Bolivia/bolivia09.html

Ellner, S. (2012). The Distinguishing Features of Latin America's New Left in Power: The Chávez, Morales and Correa Governments. *Latin American Perspectives* 38(1), 96–114.

————. (2010). Hugo Chavez's First Decade in Office: Breakthroughs and Short-comings. *Latin American Perspectives* 37(1), 77–96.

Elster, J. (1998). *Deliberative Democracy*. Cambridge, UK; New York: Cambridge University Press.

Elstub, S. (2014). Mini-Publics: Issues and Cases. In Elstub and Mclaverty, *Deliberative Democracy: Issues and Cases*. Edinburgh: Edinburgh University Press.

Elstub, S., & McLaverty, P. (2014). Issues and Cases in Deliberative Democracy. In Elstub and Mclaverty, *Deliberative Democracy: Issues and Cases*. Edinburgh: Edinburgh University Press.

Epstein, D. (1986). The Federalist. *Society 24*(1), 16–18.

Fearon, J. (1998). Deliberation as Discussion. In *Deliberative Democracy*. Cambridge, UK; New York: Cambridge University Press.

Font, J., & Galais, C. (2011). The Qualities of Local Participation: The Explanatory Role of Ideology, External Support and Civil Society as Organizer. *International Journal of Urban and Regional Research 35*(5), 932–48.

Font, J., & Smith, G. (2013). The Policy Effects of Participation. Paper presented at XI Congreso de la AECPA, Sevilla, 18–20 September.

Fung, A. (2011). Reinventing Democracy in Latin America. *Perspectives on Politics 9*(4).

————. (2007). Democratic Theory and Political Science: A Pragmatic Method of Constructive Engagement. *American Political Science Review 101*(3), 443.

————. (2006). Varieties of Participation in Complex Governance. *Public Administration Review 66*, 65–74.

Fung, A., & Wright, Olin E. (2003). *Deepening Democracy: Institutional Innovations in Empowered Participatory Governance*. London; New York: Verso.

Gallie, W. B. (1955). Essentially Contested Concepts. *Proceedings of the Aristotelian Society*, 56, 167–98.

García-Guadilla, M. (2008). La praxis de los consejos comunales en Venezuela: ¿Poder popular o instancia clientelar? *Revista Venezolana de Economía y Ciencias Sociales*, *14*(1), 125–51.

Gaventa, J. (1999). Citizen Knowledge, Citizen Competence and Democracy Building. In *Citizen Competence and Democratic Institutions*, Philadelphia: Pennsylvania State University Press, 49–65.

Gill, B., Rocamora, J., & Wilson, R. (1993). *Low Intensity Democracy: Political Power in the New World Order*, London: Pluto Press.

Goldfrank, B. (2011). *Deepening Local Democracy in Latin America: Participation, Decentralization, and the Left*. University Park: Pennsylvania State University Press.

————. (2011b). Los Consejos Comunales: ¿Avance o retroceso para la democracia venezolana? *Íconos. Revista de Ciencias Sociales*, 39, 41–55.

Habermas, J. (1984). *Theory of Communicative Action*. Boston: Beacon Press.

Hagopian, F. (2007). Latin American Citizenship and Democratic Theory. In Tulchin and Ruthenburg, eds. *Citizenship in Latin America*. Boulder, CO: Lynne Rienner Publishers.

————. (2005). Government Performance, Political Representation and Public Perceptions of Contemporary Democracy in Latin America. In Hagopian and Mainwaring. *Third Wave of Democratization in Latin America: Advances and Setbacks*. Cambridge; MA: Cambridge University Press.

————. (1990). Democracy by Undemocratic Means? Elites, political pacts, and regime transition in Brazil. *Comparative Political Studies* 23, 147–70.

Hawkins, K. (2010). Who mobilizes? Participatory Democracy in Chavez's Bolivarian Revolution. *Latin American Politics and Society,* *52*(3), 31–66.

Held, D. (2006). *Models of Democracy*. Stanford, CA: Stanford University Press.

Hellinger, D. (2011). Defying the Iron Law of Oligarchy I: How does "El Pueblo" Conceive Democracy? In Smilde, D., & Hellinger, D., *Venezuela's Bolivarian Democracy: Participation, Politcs and Culture Under Chávez*. Durham, NC: Duke University Press.

Hetland, G. (2014). The Crooked Line: From Populist Mobilization to Participatory Democracy in Chávez-era Venezuela. *Qualitative Sociology* 37(4), 373–401.

Humphreys, M., Masters, W., & Sandbu, M. (2006). The Role of Leaders in Democratic Deliberations: Results from a Field Experiment in Sao Tome and Principe. *World Politics* 58(4), 583–622.

IAP2. (2007). *IAP2 Spectrum of Public Participation.* Thornton, CO: International Association for Public Participation.

Irazabal, C., & Foley, J. (2010). Reflections on the Venezuelan Transition from a Capitalist Representative to a Socialist Participatory Democracy: What are Planners to Do? *Latin American Perspectives, 37*(1), 97–122.

Kahan, A. (2010). *Alexis de Tocqueville.* New York: Continuum.

Karl, T. L. (1990). Dilemmas of Democratization in Latin America. *Comparative Politics 23(1).*

Kaufman, Arnold S. (1969). Human Nature and Participatory Democracy. In Connolly, W. ed., *The Bias of Pluralism.* NY: Atherton Press.

Kobylka, J., & Carter, B. (1987). Madison, the Federalist, and the Constitutional Order: Human Nature and Institutional Structure. *Polity 20*(2), 190.

Lemos, R. (1978). *Hobbes and Locke: Power and Consent.* Athens: University of Georgia Press.

Lijphart, A. (1997). Unequal Participation: Democracy's Unresolved Dilemma. *American Political Science Review 91*(1), 1–14.

Linz, J., & Stepan, A. (1996). *Problems of Democratic Transition and Consolidation.* Baltimore, MD: John Hopkins University Press.

Lipset, S. (1960). *Political Man: the Social Bases of Politics.* Garden City, NY: Doubleday & Co.

López Valladares, M. (2008). Una estrategia de innovación política en Venezuela: los Consejos Comunales. *Ra Ximhai: Revista de Sociedad, Cultura, y Desarrollo Sustentable, 4*(3), 559–79.

Lovera, A. (2008). Los consejos comunales en Venezuela: ¿Democracia participativa o delegativa? *Revista Venezolana de Economía y Ciencias Sociales, 14*(1), 107–24.

Lupien, P. (2016). Radical" Participatory Democracy Institutions: Strengthening Civil Society or Mechanisms for Controlled Inclusion? In Yovanovich, G. and R. Rice, *Re-Imagining Community and Civil Society.* London: Routledge Press.

Machado, J. (2009). Participación social y consejos comunales en Venezuela. *Revista Venezolana de Economía y Ciencias Sociales, 15*(1), 173–85.

———. (2008). *Estudio de los Consejos Comunales en Venezuela.* Caracas: Fundación Centro Gumilla.

Macpherson, C. B. (1977). *Life and times of liberal democracy.* Oxford: Oxford University Press.

Mansbridge, J. (1980). *Beyond Adversary Democracy.* New York: Basic Books.

Marín, T., & Mlynarz, D. (2012). *Monitoreo a la normativa de participación ciudadana y transparencia municipal en Chile, 2012.* Santiago: Ciudad Viva.

McCarthy, M. (2012). The Possibilities and Limits of Politicized Participation: Community Councils, Coproduction, and Poder Popular in Chávez's Venezuela.

In Cameron, Hershberg, and Sharpe *New Institutions for Participatory Democracy in Latin America*. New York: Palgrave McMillian.

Mendez, C., & Jonnathan, E. (2009). Participación Ciudadana en el marco de la Constitución de la Republica Bolivariana de Venezuela y los Consejos Comunales. *Provincia,* 21, 43–60.

Migdal, J. (2001). *State-in-Society: Studying How States and Societies Transform and Constitute One Another.* New York: Cambridge University Press.

Montambeault, F. (2015). *The Politics of Local Participatory Democracy in Latin America.* Stanford, CA: Stanford University Press.

———. (2011). Overcoming Clientelism through Local Participatory Institutions in Mexico: What Type of Participation? *Latin American Politics and Society,* 53(1), 91–124.

Montero, A., & Samuels, D. (2004). *Decentralization and Democracy in Latin America.* Notre Dame, IN: University of Notre Dame Press.

Motta, S. (2009). Venezuela: Reinventing Social Democracy from Below? In Lievesley, G. and Ludlam, S. *Reclaiming Latin America: Experiments in Radical Social Democracy.* London; New York: Zed.

Mouffe, C. (1992). *Dimensions of Radical Democracy: Pluralism, Citizenship, Community.* London: Verso.

Nabatchi, T. (2012). *A Manager's Guide to Evaluating Citizen Participation* Washington, DC: IMB Center for the Business of Government.

Nelson, B. (2006). *The Making of the Modern State.* New York: Palgrave McMillian.

Nichols, M. (1992). *Citizens and Statesmen: A Study of Aristotle's Politics.* Savage, MD: Rowman & Littlefield Publishers.

Nylen, W. (2011). Participatory Institutions in Latin America: The Next Generation of Scholarship. *Comparative Politics* 40(4), 479–97.

O'Donnell, G. (2010). *Democracy, Agency, and the State: Theory with Comparative Intent.* Oxford; New York: Oxford University Press.

———. (2004). Human Development, Human Rights and Democracy. In O'Donnell, Vargas Cullel, & Iazzetta. *Quality of Democracy: Theory and Applications.* Notre Dame, IN: University of Notre Dame Press.

———. (1996). Illusions About Consolidation. *Journal of Democracy* 7(2), 34–51.

———. (1994). Delegative Democracy, *Journal of Democracy* 5(1), 55–68.

Oxhorn, P. (2016). Civil Society from the Inside Out: Community, Organization and the Challenge of Political Influence? In Yovanovich, G., & R. Rice, *Re-Imagining Community and Civil Society.* London: Routledge Press.

———. (2009). *Citizenship as Consumption or Citizenship as Agency Comparing Democratizing Reforms in Bolivia and Brazil.* Paper prepared for presentation at the annual meeting of the American Political Science Association, Toronto, September 2009.

———. (1995). *Organizing Civil Society: The Popular Sectors and the Struggle for Democracy in Chile.* University Park: Pennsylvania State University Press.

Pateman, C. (1970). *Participation and democratic theory.* Cambridge, UK: Camabridge University Press, 1974.

Petkoff, T. (2005). Las dos izquierdas. *Nueva Sociedad,* 197.

Posner, P. (2003). Local Democracy and Popular Participation: Chile and Brazil in Comparative Perspective. *Democratization 10*(3), 39–67.

Poulantzas, N. (1978). *State, Power, Socialism.* London: NLB.

Ramírez, F., & Welp, Y. (2011). Nuevas instituciones participativas y democráticas en América Latina, *Íconos. Revista de Ciencias Sociales,* 39, 41–55.

Richardson, A. (1983). *Participation.* London: Routledge.

Rivera-Ottenberger, A. (2009). Against All Odds: Participatory Local Governance and the Urban Poor in Chile. In Selee and Peruzzotti. *Participatory Innovation and Representative Democracy in Latin America.* Washington, DC: Woodrow Wilson Center Press.

Rousseau, J. J. (1994). *The Social Contract.* Oxford; NY: Oxford University Press.

Rowe, G., & Frewer, L. (2005). A Typology of Public Engagement Mechanisms, *Science, Technology and Human Value 30*(2), 251–90.

———. (2000). Public Participation Methods: A Framework for Evaluation, *Science, Technology and Human Value 25*(1), 3–29.

Santos, B. (1998). Participatory Budgeting in Porto Alegre: Toward a Redistributive Democracy, *Politics and Society, 26*(4), 461–510.

Santos, B., & Avritzer, L. (2005). Opening up the Cannon of Democracy. In *Democratizing Democracy: Beyond the Liberal Democratic Canon. Reinventing Social Emancipation.* London; New York: Verso.

Schnieder, C., & Welp, Y. (2011). ¿Transformación democrática o control político? Análisis comparado de la participación ciudadana institucional en América del Sur, *Íconos. Revista de Ciencias Sociales,* 39, 41–55.

Schumpeter, J. (1950). *Capitalism, Socialism, and Democracy.* New York: Harper.

Seawright, J., & Gerring, J. (2008). Case Selection Techniques in Case Study Research. *Political Research Quarterly, 61*(2), 294–308.

Selee, A., & Peruzzotti, E. (2009). *Participatory Innovation and Representative Democracy in Latin America.* Washington, DC: Woodrow Wilson Center Press.

Selee, A. (2009). An Alternative to Clientelism? Participatory Innovation in Mexico. In Selee and Peruzzotti. *Participatory Innovation and Representative Democracy in Latin America.* Washington, DC: Woodrow Wilson Center Press.

Smilde, D. (2011). Introduction. In Smilde and Hellinger, *Venezuela's Bolivarian Democracy: Participation, Politcs and Culture Under Chávez.* Durham, NC: Duke University Press.

Smith, G. (2009). *Democratic Innovations: Designing Institutions for Citizen Participation.* Cambridge, UK; New York: Cambridge University Press.

Smith, P. (2012). *Democracy in Latin America: Political Change in Comparative Perspective.* New York: Oxford University Press.

Snyder, R. (2001). Scaling Down: The Subnational Comparative Method. *Studies in Comparative International Development, 36*(1), 93–110.

Sunstein, C. (2003). *Why Societies Need Dissent*. Cambridge, MA: Harvard University Press.

Tocqueville, A. (1994). *Democracy in America*. New York: A. Knopf: Distributed by Random House.

Urribarri, R. (2008). Venezuela—The Left Turning Further Left? In *Leftovers: Tales of the Two Latin American Lefts*. London: Routledge, 174–92.

Van Cott, D. L. (2008). *Radical Democracy in the Andes*. Cambridge, UK; New York: Cambridge University Press.

Venezuela, República bolivariana de. (2009). *Proyecto de Ley de Reforma de la Ley de los Consejos Comunales*. http://www.alcaldiagirardot.gob.ve/consejoscomunales/reforma_ley_consejos.pdf

———. (2006). *Ley de los Consejos Comunales*. http://gp.cnti.ve/site/minpades.gob.ve/view/documentoShow.php?id=24

———. (1999). *Constitución Bolivariana de la República de Venezuela*. http://gp.cnti.ve/site/minpades.gob.ve /view/documentoShow.php?id=29

Wampler, B. (2007). *Participatory Budgeting in Brazil: Contestation, Cooperation and Accountability*. University Park: Pennsylvania State University Press.

Warren, M. (1996). What should we expect from more democracy? Radically democratic responses to politics. *Political Theory 24*(2), 241–70.

Williams, D. (2007). *Rousseau's Platonic Enlightenment*. University Park: Pennsylvania State University Press.

Yashar, D. (2007). Resistance and Identity Politics in an Age of Globalization. *The Annals of the American Academy of Political and Social Science 610*(1), 160–81.

———. (2005). *Contesting citizenship in Latin America: the Rise of Indigenous Movements and the Postliberal Challenge*. Cambridge; New York: Cambridge University Press.

Zamosc, L. (2004). The Indian Movement in Ecuador: From Politics of Influence to Politics of Power. In *Struggle for Indigenous Rights in Latin America*. Brighton, UK; Portland, OR: Sussex Academic Press.

Index